THE SILENT CHILD IN ME

MICHELLE ENSUQUE

SilverWood

Published in 2023 by SilverWood Books

SilverWood Books Ltd
14 Small Street, Bristol, BS1 1DE, United Kingdom
www.silverwoodbooks.co.uk

Text copyright © Michelle Ensuque 2023

The right of Michelle Ensuque to be identified as the author of this
work has been asserted in accordance with the Copyright,
Designs and Patents Act 1988 Sections 77 and 78.

All rights reserved. No part of this publication may be reproduced,
stored in a retrieval system, or transmitted in any form or by any means,
electronic, mechanical, photocopying, recording or otherwise,
without prior permission of the copyright holder.

This is a work of fiction. Names, characters, places and incidents either
are products of the author's imagination or are used fictitiously. Any
resemblance to actual events or locales or persons,
living or dead, is entirely coincidental.

ISBN 978-1-80042-220-9 (paperback)

British Library Cataloguing in Publication Data
A CIP catalogue record for this book is
available from the British Library

Page design and typesetting by SilverWood Books

MICHELLE ENSUQUE is a behavioural coach whose project management and consultant career has spanned 30 years across public and private sectors. Michelle suffered a breakdown around 10 years ago which was a shock as she always believed her zest for life, energy and sense of humour would get her through most things but, balancing the needs of family as a single parent coupled with a demanding job and other life events, such as bereavement, eventually took its toll.

Michelle spent 12 months working on her recovery, a big part of which was Neuro Linguistic Programming which completely transformed her life, both personally and professionally.

She wasn't aware of how she was operating, her patterns of behaviour that led to her driving herself relentlessly and why, ultimately, at an emotional level she ended up at rock bottom.

Michelle now works with people in the corporate world, who are trying to balance the professional with the personal and helps them too (and often their families), to make transformational changes. Her mission is to help people potentially avoid the mental health issues that ravage our society. Many examples are given in this book to help people understand what might be triggering certain behaviours through the story and some thought provoking questions to aid the reader into questioning their current mode of operating.

Her website is www.meliusse.com and she can often be found scribing hilarious posts on LinkedIn https://www.linkedin.com/in/meliusseuk

Dedicated to my grandad for giving me the gift of love, so that I knew what it looked like and could hold on to it. Even if it felt like the briefest moment in time.

This book contains information about trauma, abuse, suicide and eating disorders.

As I look back now at the silent child in me
I see frightened eyes and fear where joy should be.
I didn't know it then, but fear would have the last laugh,
As later it pulled me down an ever-spiralling path.

There at the bottom I looked up at a wall of grey,
No sky at the top to welcome, no sense of light or day.
Was I in this life or the next, I wondered? It mattered not, I thought,
As my fingers scrabbled on the surface, as a way out of there was sought.

The climb was long and heavy and not without some pain,
But finally, I reached the top and gone was my shame.
The shame of imperfection, of not being good enough
Was replaced by something other, more resilient and tough.

To my silent child I say, you were stronger than you knew,
Your defiant stance and bravery were the very essence of you.
I love you, my silent child, for dealing with all that pain,
Tell your story to the world so others don't endure the same.

Michelle Ensuque

Chapter 1

Grandad, I Love You

Oi, you! Yes, you! I can see you turning the page back to see if you're in the right place. What? No prologue? No long introduction where I'm supposed to give thanks to my loved ones, my hairdresser, the dog groomer or my acupuncturist for giving me the inspiration or support in writing this? Nope, we are here, cutting to the chase, getting down to the real stuff from page one. If you're like me, I barely read those prologues anyway. I just want to get to the story! So, with that out of the way, I'm Michelle. Nice to meet you. Are you ready to begin?

It was time to leave. Nothing weird about that. The holiday was over and it was time to go home. So I set about packing. I had a faint feeling of déjà vu but wasn't quite sure why, and then realised the time. Dammit! The transport will leave soon! It was 4.20pm on my watch and the bus was leaving at 4.40pm, but there was so much to do. There were two huge suitcases, big black ones, soft and squishy. But packing everything required it all to be sorted if I was to fit everything in. But why was that the case if I hadn't really bought anything? I thought, why didn't

I sort all this last night? Still, methodically I went through the items, putting them in 'to leave' or 'to take' piles, until suddenly I noticed it was 4.50pm. No! Running downstairs, I yanked one of the suitcases with me; it bumped down each step, nearly pushing me over in the process. I was half-hoping I would still see my friends waiting. But no, of course not. Where they should have been were just empty chairs. Empty packets wafted in the breeze – packets that had once contained a hot dog bursting out of its doughy cushion, remnants of sauce still remaining on the paper, mustard and tomato colour. Why hadn't they called me to see where I was? That struck me as not very kind. There was nothing and no one outside either; everything seemed eerily quiet, which in itself was odd because I was in Delhi, where nothing stood still or was quiet – at least, not for very long.

Suddenly my heart was pounding. I started to panic, but just as I did, I opened my eyes, shot bolt upright and realised that it was just a dream. The relief! Slumping back down into my pillows, I pondered the fact that it wasn't the first time I had dreamed this scenario. The location might have been different, but it was the same story. I wondered what the oneirologists or Freud would say about that. Anyway, that day I decided to do something different. To return to the same place, but this time I wanted to change the ending of the dream to something far more positive. After all, if it was in my head, I could do that, couldn't I? Settling down, I took myself back to the point just before I had woken up. I was in the bedroom. I threw everything into the suitcases, went downstairs, got on the transport and travelled to the airport. I was still alone, but this was much better than the other ending. There was an old couple in front of me in the queue, and although I could feel the dream trying to introduce things like 'Is this the right airport, or the right queue?' I batted them away like flies and maintained my focus. Now I felt much safer, much surer of the direction of travel and, more importantly, in control. While I didn't see myself arriving home, I felt safe enough to open my eyes and return to the real world, knowing the one I'd left behind was just fine. If only life could be like that, where you could rewind and create a more positive outcome, I thought. Well, later in life I would be able to do just that, but at this point there was only one ending, and it wasn't a good one. There are some things, after all, that you can't change.

The rain was pouring down the glass. The inside of the coach window was steamy. The air was damp and heavy, full of people's warm bodies and wet clothes from standing outside in the rain. There was lots of excited chatter as people discussed where they were going. I sat there in my little red coat and hat as we waited to depart for the trip. Swinging my legs back and forth, I took a sneaky peak sideways at the man sat next to me. He had a pointy nose and his chin poked out. It was a strong look, but I never got tired of it. "I never want you to die, Grandad." "Don't you?" he smiled. And with that he was gone. One minute we were on the bus, off on a day trip together, and the next he had disappeared from my life. I was nine. How was that actually possible? I thought. Had he been abducted by aliens? I had heard about such things and it seemed entirely possible; I mean, I didn't know anyone else who had just disappeared into thin air. People talked about it, but it just seemed silly. There was something else 'off', though. A bit like a bad smell that you didn't know where it was coming from but you kept searching for it because you knew the answer was somewhere. This was like that. There were also people toing and froing from our house. I giggled. This shouldn't be unusual, but in this house no one really visited, apart from those who lived in it (and I'm not sure even they wanted to be there) and a few family members. My other grandad cycled round sometimes on Sundays and said he was off to the church where they had handles on the prayer books. For years I hadn't understood it, especially as he had never uttered anything religious in his life, until one day the realisation of where he was actually going lined up like fruit on a slot machine. Anyway, the comings and goings made me thoughtful. There must be something going on. Obviously I was just a kid; there was no need for me to know. Out of sight, out of mind.

There was a vague memory of being told Grandad had died – a heart attack, apparently – but it was one of those memories I couldn't quite touch. Don't give me that twaddle about it being so far in the past. A smell or song could ricochet me back into an old memory in a nanosecond. No, this was the realisation that this was such a bad memory the brain had decided to store it so deep that no one could find it. That way, if you can't find it, it can't hurt, right?

On the day of the funeral, I went to school like any other day. My parents must have told the school what had happened, as rather unusually I found myself sitting on my teacher's knee. He was talking away, probably about how death was natural and a process for old people, but really it was like his lips were moving but there was no sound. I looked round at everyone else in the room. Did I really know any of these kids? Even now I can't picture a single one of them. Did they actually care about what I was thinking or feeling? Right now, who was actually with me? No one. As per normal. As an only child, life pretty much existed in my own head. Not in an invisible friend kind of way, but in a 'this is enough' kind of way. Anyway, I sat on his lap for what felt like ages, but all I felt was the scratchiness of his trousers on my legs and all I could see were his glasses wobbling on his face as he talked. I wanted to giggle, but that seemed inappropriate. I struggled to remember his name. Was it Mr Waring? He was my favourite teacher, always praising me, telling me he loved my story writing, and I was so proud I thought my heart might burst. Compliments were few and far between, so I took what I got.

So he might have been talking about my grandad but, honestly, it might as well have been about the weather. I wondered if I ought to be at school at all, and thought vaguely that maybe I should be somewhere else. Later I understood that my parents considered I was too young to go to the funeral; but I was nine, not dumb. I knew that I had needed to see it for myself in order to accept it. The suddenness of it (it wasn't the last time I would experience someone's sudden death) and not seeing his coffin left an imprint of disbelief, of thinking that he actually hadn't died. That it was all a lie and any time now I would see him walk up our driveway, or that he would meet me outside school on Wednesdays, just like he used to. For years afterwards I saw his face in a crowd, and every time I did it made me catch my breath – my heart fluttered and my stomach somersaulted with joy, and then seconds later it plummeted when I realised it wasn't him after all. It was like those first few seconds when you wake up, having forgotten a tragic event, thinking it was all a dream, before, two seconds later, reality kicks in. There was no changing this dream, though. I hadn't just lost my grandad; I had lost my safe place.

Closing my eyes, I could warp myself back to his house in a split second – the place where, from about six to nine years of age, I felt most loved; where there was calmness, peace and tranquillity and an open fire. For hours I used to love watching that fire, the open flames flickering. There was no TV, but that was OK. There was the fire, happiness and love in abundance. Not the sicky-icky kind that comes gushing out every five minutes, but just a 'knowing' that love existed. In this house, unlike the one I shared with my parents, there was no shouting, no awkward painful silences and, most importantly, no fear. I felt relaxed, and every time I walked over the threshold I let out a huge breath and felt my shoulders relax and the knot in my tummy release.

The journey to his house for those week-long holidays was hilarious. He had this immaculate Ford Anglia. Was it grey or lilac? Not sure, but it was pristine. He absolutely refused to drive more than 40mph and I used to silently giggle at the queue behind as he drove onwards, oblivious. They are strange, aren't they – memories? There are the ones I pushed away, because remembering them caused too much pain, and yet there were others I could recall as though I had experienced them the day before. Such as running upstairs to get a book from the bookcase that was on top of the landing: Enid Blyton, the Brothers Grimm fairy tales, Agatha Christie, Inspector Poirot. My favourite place in the whole house was his armchair – still much loved and now decadently covered in rich purple velvet – in the lounge. When I wasn't sewing in that chair, I was reading those books I found in the bookcase. I feasted on them, absorbing words like a sponge. When I read, it was like there was a movie in my head. Later in life, in my thirties, this trait proved rather irritating, as reading the Harry Potter books before the movies came out was a big mistake. Huge! It was as though every detail was already imprinted on my mind in glorious Technicolor, so it was like watching the movie for the second time.

My reading was more successful than my sewing. I tried to remember if I had ever actually made anything. There was a faint memory of a cotton bobbin with four little nails in the top and of spending hours winding the wool round and pulling it through like a knitted sausage. The little things that brought pleasure, which now, as I type a message to a friend on my phone, feels ancient in its very being. Those days weren't without some pain, but generally they were self-inflicted, such as accidentally jamming my hand onto a needle when I had decided to use the arm of the chair as a kind of pincushion. Screaming and running out to the kitchen to where Grandad was, with my hand outstretched, all I wanted was someone to take the pain away. Grandad did that. He was so scared that day; his face as I came bursting through the kitchen door…but relief when he understood why, as later he told me that he thought I had stuck my hand in the fire. Very gently he pulled out the needle; he was always so tender and softly spoken.

If you were to ask me now what meals he made for me, I couldn't give you a single example. I found it hilarious that he always made a cup of tea with sugar in. Yuk. My mum was diabetic, so there was never any sugar in the house, and definitely not in tea, but he seemed oblivious to this, and as he was so perfect in every way I always let it slide. Plus if I said I wasn't allowed to have sugar, the secret stash of chocolate buttons that appeared every time I visited might have disappeared too. So I was not going to argue over a bit of sugar in my tea. If you argued about something, there was always a consequence – although I can't imagine what kind of consequence my grandad would have dished out – but I kept my lips firmly shut anyway, just in case. When the chocolate buttons did make their entrance – silently, stealthily just 'appearing' on the table – I would move them next to the fireplace. Every now and then I would give the bag a squeeze, and as if on cue Grandad brought in a teaspoon to spoon out the warm, gooey decadence. Oh, my word. The beauty of it. Forty-nine years later I can still feel the beauty of that moment and the melted chocolate oozing on my tongue. It was magical.

My biggest regret is not asking Grandad any questions about his life. Only when I was being yanked round every posh house in the country after his death did I realise that he used to be a butler to Winston Churchill and other eminent lords and ladies. How could I not know something as big as this? Later on, I would look at my relationship with my own children and realise they didn't ask questions about my life either. Why would they, when theirs hadn't yet started and the anticipation of what was to come was exciting? I mean, I'm 'old' – everyone over forty (OK, thirty) is old, so my life would seem quite boring in comparison; plus, for most of the experiences, you really would have had to have been there.

So, grandparents being as old as they are (somehow I never thought he would die, despite being ancient), how could their lives be of any interest to us as children? I was listening to Helena Bonham Carter the other day. I think she is the one who lived in a house next door to her husband. You know the one? Skinny actress. Hauntingly beautiful, like a female Johnny Depp. She was a guest on Louis Theroux's podcast and was explaining that she had completed a documentary, interviewing older people – mainly her family – and said she thought all grandchildren should interview their grandparents. What a fabulous idea! I thought about that for a moment; but, with no assistance, I think my questions would have probably revolved around: 'What do you do when I am not with you? If you don't have a job, why do you only come to our house on Wednesdays?' (I still say 'Wed-nes-days' in my head every time I write it out. Is that weird?) 'Why don't you have any teeth? Why do you drive so slowly? How did you learn to make a fire out of such small bits of newspaper?' And all manner of other trivial things. Would any of those answers (with the exception of the fire making) elicit a response around being a butler for the gentry? Besides, I'm not sure I would even have known who Mr Churchill was.

Once more I cast my mind back to my young self in Grandad's house. Every night, before I went to sleep, I used to think about the same thing. The sound of the ticking, chiming clock. In his house it was just a clock, but after his death – when it was transferred to our mantlepiece – my mum suggested that the clock signified the death of others. It would stop ticking and then randomly start. Three days later someone would die. It wasn't just one event; apparently it had happened a few times. I wondered where the clock went. Had my mum got sick of being reminded about death and got rid of it? I remembered the smell of the old furniture and the old books. The bed I shared with him, the red satin eiderdown and the fact he used to take his teeth out and plop them in the glass of water next to the bed. The way I always used to force him to speak without his teeth, which made me giggle uncontrollably, so of course he talked even more. The innocence of it all. The laughter. The love. Then realising that those things would never happen any more, and death meant that was final. I wondered if he had been dressed in the coffin. Did he have underpants on? Why did I even worry about his underpants? It wasn't as if I had ever seen him get dressed or undressed. He was always somehow just – well, dressed. But what was the use of underpants if he was dead? Had they put his false teeth in so he could talk properly, or was he going to look like he'd sucked a vacuum cleaner instead? I giggled. Far better to remember the laughs and giggles than the sadness. If he was somehow able to smoke his pipe, the smell of his tobacco sweet and heavy, could he do that once he was dead? Hilarious: the smoke coming out of the ground, seeping out of the cracks, scaring someone witless on Halloween. All of these things floated in and out of my mind.

After that, there was nothing…except a silence of a different kind. The silence that hangs over death like a heavy mist. It was a bit like going downstairs and finding that everyone had left me behind, leaving nothing but food wrappers. It was time to build a fortress, I thought. I could hear myself muttering, "I've lost my safe place," so the creation of another was necessary. If you were to ask me now if I remember doing that, you would see my puzzled expression. It just kind of happened.

There was another house where there was silence, a feeling of dread, where even ghosts would cower in the corner wondering if it was safe to make an entrance. The house always appeared melancholy and had a bad vibe. On my way home from school I always approached it with fear, never knowing what to expect. It might as well have been a haunted house, because no one wanted to go there. I had to. I lived there.

What might this mean for you?

- If you knew your grandparents, how did they impact your life?

- If your grandparents are still alive, what questions would you love to ask them?

- How has bereavement affected you (no matter when it occurred) and what steps have you taken to overcome its impact?

- What are your role models for love and relationships, and what impact have they had on the way you think or act with others?

- If you have had trauma in your early years, how has that impacted you? How have you coped with its effects and what help have you sought to move forward and truly enjoy your life?

Chapter 2

Mirror, Mirror on the Wall

My reflection stared back at me
Mocking, yet sad
What did I do to deserve such a fate?
Surely, I wasn't that bad?

So young and defiant
At least outwardly so
But inside the pain
Settled like winter snow

They could punish me all they wanted
But inside I knew very well
It was not me who was evil
It was they who lived in hell

Michelle Ensuque

I woke with a jump, a loud clapping of hands and the call of "Rise and shine." My alarm clock was my dad. There was no easy wake-up. No gentle shove on the shoulder or a cup of tea.

No, it was a military-esque rude awakening, although that probably proved useful in later years. Every morning was the same for as long as I could remember, and every night, from as early as when I was five or six years of age, saw him sitting by my bed with his fingers on my eyelids, pressing them so I'd go to sleep. I didn't understand that. It just seemed weird. Did my mum press his eyes shut to go to sleep? If she did that for him, who pressed hers? I never argued – that was pointless. I never questioned it. That was also pointless. I just did as I was told and went to sleep.

Did as I was told. That pretty much summed up my childhood. "I say jump, you say 'how high?'" was the motto in our house. Nothing was ever good enough. I wasn't good enough. "You are ugly, stupid, fat," were frequent words used, so today was nothing abnormal.

"That is hideous!" barked Dad, pointing his finger in my direction. Great, here we go again, I thought. Same old record.

"I mean, look at that thing on your lip, it's disgusting." I knew it was disgusting. I didn't have to be told it. A scab had formed on my lip – a cold sore, apparently, although I had no idea what it was at the time. Also, I had 'apparently' manifested this on purpose, just to annoy him. "I tell you, if that thing is still there tomorrow, you aren't going on the school trip. I'm not having any child of mine looking like that."

I felt the familiar shame and recoil as I stood in front of the mirror. How on earth was I going to get rid of that by tomorrow? It was the size of my pinkie nail! It stood out like a huge carbuncle on my little lips; honestly, I thought spots were bad enough. But I simply had to go on the school trip. It was a day away from this place, where for just one day I could forget everything. I was damned if I was going to lose out because of something that wasn't my fault. So later, upstairs in the bathroom, bit by bit I picked it off. I pursed my lips shut to prevent me crying out, but my eyes filled with tears as it smarted every time I got hold of a bit and pulled. But I was also excited because it was actually coming off! Finally it was done. It hurt but it was worth it. There was a little bit of pink skin, but the ugly scab had gone. I was a bit concerned it might grow back overnight, but I would take that chance.

The next morning, I went downstairs. He stared at me and grumped, "It's gone, then," and walked off. I did a little internal fist pump and felt triumphant. Yes! I was going on the school trip. I could feel his irritation that I had thwarted him, that there were no more excuses to be nasty. Not this time, anyway – I had escaped. There was a fleeting thought that my mum might actually have tried to stick up for me, but no, she was silent, as per usual. Thanks for that, I thought. Today, though, I could go and have fun, escape and forget this place for a few precious hours.

I couldn't work out what I had done that was so wrong. Dad actually sat me down one day and said: "You know, I was so looking forward to having a child, and then you came along and I was so disappointed to have you as a daughter. Why can't you look like Alison, my god-daughter? She is really pretty and funny."

That hurt. To the core. I mean, I couldn't help how I looked. I'd look in the mirror and wonder what I could do to make myself better. I wasn't even sure I would become perfect even if I tried. That felt too way off. It's true, Alison was naturally pretty, but I couldn't become someone else. I was simply me.

I was distracted for a moment by raised voices downstairs. Again. I couldn't wait to get out of here. Could…not…wait.

I ran down the stairs, picked up my bag and ran out of the house to catch the bus. Freedom for a day! It was to prove short-lived.

"Right," he shouted, "that's it, I'm taking you to the doctor's. You are too fat. We will see what he says."

I sighed. This again. My weight and size had been an issue for as long as I could remember. But I ate what they gave me, and of course the principle was that you had to eat everything on your plate, and you had to eat quickly. If I ate too slowly, he barked because he had to wait for his pudding, and he didn't like waiting for anything. I walked or cycled everywhere – to school and back, out in the countryside for miles at the weekend – and still nothing worked. Little did I know that this feeling of being big, and the all the issues surrounding it, would last an entire lifetime; but right now, despite my annoyance that my size and appearance had somehow come to the top of the list of discussions again, someone was going to fix it.

The doctor peered at me over his glasses, his hand poised with a pen over his pad. I listened to Dad droning on about my weight. Well, in truth I didn't hear much. I just stared in front of me. No one asked me any questions or for my view. After all, I was just a child, fourteen years of age, so what did I know? I was acutely aware of my body changes thank you, and sitting here hearing them talking like this was humiliating. The subject of what I looked like and how 'disappointing' that was – it was not just the topic of conversation behind four walls, it was now 'out there'. So I tried to tune everything out and pretend I wasn't there. But wait – what did the doctor say? He could help? I was stunned. He had a cure! He was going to take this issue away once and for all. It wasn't my fault. He saw that, and he was going to give me something to fix it. This was turning out better than expected! He scribbled furiously on his notepad, tore the top sheet off and gave the prescription to my dad. "Appetite suppressants," he said looking at me, "so you won't feel hungry." I did a little dance in my head. I could see myself becoming svelte, slim, the image of loveliness my dad wanted, and along with it would come love and pride, replacing disappointment and disgust. My self-loathing would disappear; I would be more popular at school, have more friends. I might even be able to bag myself a boyfriend. Skipping out of the surgery, we stopped off to get the medication. Little did I know things were about to get a whole lot worse.

Interestingly, this time it started off being about respect. Ha! Like anyone in this house knew the meaning of such a word. Even down to my room. Apparently it was not *my* room. It was *their* room. It was theirs to do what they wanted with, to walk into whenever they wanted. While I lived in their house, I lived under their rules and regulations. That was the deal, that's what they said. My mum would constantly say: "If you want to treat the place like a hotel, go and live in one." I'm not sure I really understood what that meant, considering my age, but I was positive hotels were actually much nicer than my own home. The bedroom furniture couldn't be moved. If I ever dared to, I'd go back later and find that, as if by magic, it was where it had originally been. There were daffodil-yellow walls, red-and-white duvet covers, a green chair. Jeez. Basically, all the colours I hated, but I hadn't been asked my opinion, so I had to accept it. The feeling of being controlled was palpable. To have no voice, no say, no sense of being, no right to anything was, at the very least, demoralising. To live in fear was exhausting. Most of the time I felt like a frightened deer, constantly on the lookout for danger, holding myself tight, ready to flee at any moment. Later, much later, a homeopath would tell me that it was unsurprising I had suffered from constant constipation, holding myself so tight. I'd never thought of it like that.

Today, though – today was a day to flee. "Why aren't you eating your supper?" Dad shouted.

I was utterly confused. I was deliriously happy because the pills were working. I didn't feel hungry. As a result, I was struggling to eat the meal on my plate. The plate where my mum had served up the food, like always, and it was a Monday. Every Monday was the same – leftover roast meat (cold) and warm vegetables. Hardly Michelin cuisine, but it was at least edible.

"I just don't feel hungry, Dad," I replied.

"You will eat what your mother has put in front of you."

"You can't have it both ways, Dad. On the one hand you want me to lose weight and on the other you want me to eat all my food. Which is it?" The words had leapt out of my mouth before I'd had even registered what I'd said, and it was too late. By the time I'd seen the look on my dad's face, the damage was done. I knew what was coming. It was like a switch had been flicked. He would later, perhaps when I was in my twenties, describe it as being like a red mist coming down where he couldn't see anything. It was supposed to be some sort of explanation.

Whack! I barely saw it coming. The back of the hand across my face that hit so hard I toppled off the stool and fell back against the dining room door. His face was livid, the anger filled the air. Over what? Some uneaten food? Really?

"Don't you ever disrespect me or your mother!" he yelled, spittle spewing from his mouth as he shouted. As if he ever respected her in the first place.

I scooted underneath his arm, but his hand shot out and caught me. As he went to punch me I ducked, and he stuck his hand through the cupboard door instead. I took the opportunity of his momentary disbelief to run upstairs as fast as I could. I ran into my room and shut the door, but of course there was no safety – there was no lock. He pushed the door open. Bam! Another backhander. This one saw me catapulting backwards over the bed, and I felt a pain in my fingers as they bent backwards on the radiator. Then they came flying – the fists and the slaps. I curled into a ball and waited for it to be over, tears silently pouring down my cheeks. Finally silence. He turned, marched out of the room and slammed the door shut. What had I done to deserve this? I was fifteen. I looked at other people's lives and wondered if they suffered the same things. No one talked about their lives behind closed doors. I imagined it was much like they made them out to be in the movies. I hate this place, I thought. Hate, hate, hate it!

On the rare occasion I was left in peace alone at home, I used to wander around the house searching for adoption papers, because I couldn't believe that real parents would treat a child this way. They would want them, right? I mean, really want them; and if they wanted them, they would love them, not hurt them. If my mum was real she would protect me, wouldn't she? In all the wildlife programmes I had seen, the mother was the fiercest protector of all with her offspring. Yet I had lost count of the times my mum had gone around the house, shutting the windows so the neighbours wouldn't hear me screaming. Oh yes, mustn't alert the neighbours to anything. Or the time on the radio when they were talking about child abuse and my mum said, "At least you can say you've never been hit," as I sat there sporting a black eye (those darn cupboard doors spring out of nowhere). I wondered how I was supposed to deal with that when the obvious was ignored, obliterated, so that everyone could pretend nothing had happened. If I told anyone, I would be branded a liar, a child with an overactive imagination. Ha! That phrase was to come back and haunt me in later years.

As I sat in my room, too scared to come out, I wondered if my dad would just finish me off one day. That way no one would have to be disappointed any more, or scared, or humiliated. After a few hours I turned the door handle, millimetre by millimetre so as to avoid highlighting my clearly unwanted presence. Finally the door opened, and I crept, Pink Panther-style, with long steps, one foot placed down silently before moving the other, towards the bathroom. I was a good girl. Never missed a day cleaning my teeth, and this wasn't going to stop me now. I crept back and crawled into bed. I couldn't bring myself to go to the toilet, for fear of drawing attention to myself. There were no 'goodnights' in this house. No 'sweet dreams', no bedtime stories; but there was comfort and relief in my bed. I had only been dragged from it a few times by my arm, so for the most part it was considered the safest part of the house. In my head, anyway. Here I could enter the world of make-believe. Imagination. I would continue the theme of finding my true parents. I quite liked one of my music teachers, who seemed very kind. She was someone who looked like they could be my mum. I constructed the story of somehow going to school and that same teacher sitting me down and telling me, "I think I'm your mum," and she would hug me and have this happy reunion. Life would be blissful, in that happy-ever-after way that only happens in fairy tales. Of course, it never happened. There was never a reunion, just this life, where there were no hugs, just rules, expectations, demands, threats, violence and overwhelming disappointment. That didn't stop me thinking that there could be something else, always hopeful that something much better was out there. It might be just beyond my reach, but one day I would touch it.

Of course, right on cue, in the early hours of the morning, my body woke me up, signalling that missing the toilet stop as part of the bedtime ritual had been a bad idea. Dammit, I thought, not now. My stomach clenched with fear as I imagined tiptoeing across the landing, not wanting to raise any awareness of me being awake, but I really needed a wee. My mind worked hard to find a way out of this, but it was impossible. It wasn't as if we were in a bungalow, with easy access outside. I had no sink in my room. It was the toilet or nothing. I thought hard again. If I did it behind the chair, would anyone notice? When was my room due to be cleaned? I tried to work out the day. Every room had a day assigned to it. My brain couldn't remember; it was too worried about being scared. Well, the fear of what might meet me on the landing far outweighed the fear of being found out, so in the dead of night, behind my chair, I peed. Relief mixed with fear over being found out, but mostly relief at this point.

It felt very devious, and I giggled in my head at the secrecy of it all. It was no laughing matter, though – not feeling safe enough to go for a pee in your own home at night – but it made me giggle nonetheless. I thought I'd got away with it, but a few days later, when I returned home from school, I realised that had just been wishful thinking. My mum had a routine. Every room was cleaned within an inch of its life and each room had a designated cleaning day. She must have moved my chair out and seen the stain, or been on her hands and knees cleaning the skirting boards. It didn't really matter how she had discovered it, to be honest; as soon as I stepped through the doorway and saw her tight pursed lips and stare I knew, and my stomach fell. I was called a slut, among other things, and when my dad returned home from work the violence rained down on me once more; the good humour I had felt before was lost on me and forgotten. What did go through my head was: why was I being beaten for this? If I could just have gone to the toilet in the dead of night like any other person (surely *they* did from time to time?), none of this would have happened. It wasn't like I had chosen to do this. I really had had no choice. Well, clearly I had, and I realised that I had made the wrong one, and while the outcome might have been the same, I wouldn't have felt so ashamed.

Finally there came a point where I broke, but not in the way I thought. Yet another argument had kicked off. I felt tired of pretending at school with my friends and teachers, wearing long-sleeved blouses to hide the burst blood vessels on my arms. Tired of never knowing from one day to the next what the atmosphere would be like at home. I'd walk home from school by the long route, just to delay the inevitable. Since my grandad's death, school was one of the only places I liked to be. I could escape the house and feel a certain sense of pride with some teachers who valued my work. That gave me a warm, fuzzy feeling inside. My mum once asked: "Why don't you behave at home like you do at school?" (Apparently they said I was happy and attentive.) My response was simple. "Because they don't treat me at school like you do at home." Words failed her at that point and she walked off.

Today I opened the door and there were raised voices. My heart sank and my stomach clenched. Here we go again, I thought. Quietly and carefully I put my school bag down in the kitchen and went to go upstairs. I didn't want to alert anyone to my presence. I would rather just slink upstairs unnoticed and seek solitude in my room until dinner. But no. As I walked past the living room door, it opened suddenly and my dad stood there, red-faced and sweating. "What the hell are you doing here skulking around, eh?"

I didn't answer. Like a cornered deer I looked left and right, considering my options.

"I asked you a question." And with that, he yanked me into the living room so hard I nearly toppled head first into the metal bars of the gas fire.

Something bubbled up inside me; I was sick of this. Sick of him. He started to shout, and suddenly I found my voice. I screamed, and kicked the footstool round the living room. It must have looked utterly hilarious. Me screaming and kicking. Round and round the lounge I went, kicking the footstool over and over while at the same time screaming my head off. My dad for once gobsmacked and silent. His eyes wide with sheer surprise. But then he changed. The shock subsided and anger took over once more. He grabbed me by the throat and pushed me up against the door so hard that my feet barely touched the floor. In that moment I sagged. It was as though life had already been taken from me. I didn't want this life. This wasn't a life, it was a living hell – and I wanted out.

"Do you know what?" he spat. "When you were born, I was so fiercely proud to have a daughter. I had all these hopes and dreams, and then you grew up and turned out nothing like I expected. It's really very disappointing."

What a surprise that I was being reminded, yet again, that I was a disappointment just by being me, I thought. I wondered who was more disappointed – him in me or me in him? My expectations of how a father should behave were also very different. When other people said, "You must be a very spoilt child because you are the only one," I snorted. The irony of it all. I hid all of it from everyone. I told no one. There was just me, in my own mind and little world. Today my world seemed tiny and inconsiderate. Very quietly I looked him in the face and said, "Do it, then. Kill me. I've had enough."

He dropped me in that moment, turned around and walked away. I was actually surprised. I had anticipated a tighter squeeze, but he'd let go. Maybe there was something nice in there after all, or at least he had registered things had gone too far. My mind was made up. I might only have been seventeen, but I knew if I stayed here it would be the death of me one way or another. So, over the coming days, I organised another place to stay in my home town and wrote a letter to my parents. It said:

"When you read this tomorrow, I will be gone. They say two is company and three is a crowd, so for the sake of the survival of this family – as you have often told me, I am the problem – I have decided to move out. I hope you will be happy."

Tears streamed down my face as I wrote. I might have wanted this, but equally this had been my home. Now I was going out into the world to fend for myself, with no idea what to expect – just, hopefully, some peace and laughter.

I wouldn't know it yet, but patterns were forming in my psyche. I'd never thought about yesterday or dwelled on previous events. However, that also meant I didn't 'deal' with them, but just pretended they had never existed. Why? Because for me every day was a new day. No one could actually do anything about what had gone on before, so what was the point in dwelling on it? When I saw myself in the mirror, all I saw was an ugly girl looking back at me. I had no right to happiness, looking like that. I deserved everything that came my way.

I deserved to be bullied at school. I was, and I didn't dare tell my parents. If I did, that would be seen as another failure, but my dad would undoubtedly deal with it, and quite possibly my bully might have met their match. There was a fleeting moment when this was actually an awesome thought – that someone else could be the punchbag for a while – but that was really mean. No; just like everything else, I would have to sort this out alone.

As an only child, I was good at sorting things out by myself. There was no one else to talk to about 'stuff', so I could either choose to drive myself mad with 'what ifs' or I could crack on. So the only person I had a conversation with was myself in my head. Besides, there were good days and good times. My life wasn't like this every day – although it's true I did live in fear every day and felt like I was walking on eggshells, wondering when things were going to go downhill. But our family had shared some laughs together too. We played Monopoly at Christmas, laughed our heads off when Mum discovered she had 'cooked' custard instead of the omelette mixture, and took the mick out of Dad with his scratched face when he had fallen into a holly bush because he was too drunk to get home from his local. Sadly, those good times were mere punctuations on the landscape of life. I thought I had learned some good things from all this: determination; strength; that I would have to work hard to succeed; and that humour could get me through most things. I had learned some things that I was not, as yet, aware of: fear of not being enough; controlling behaviour was acceptable and normal; and standing up for yourself had consequences. I couldn't connect with others easily or form attachments. Being disappointed and let down was normal.

As I settled down to sleep, I thought about how quickly things could change, how unpredictable life could be and how the next day is just that – another day where you could start over and pretend the previous one had never existed. For the first time, I thought about what was within my control to achieve. The decision I made that night – to leave this godforsaken place – would change the course of my life and make up for the somewhat shaky start.

What might this mean for you?

- In terms of self-belief, what do you believe about yourself? If you were to insert words after 'I am…', what would they be?

- When you look in the mirror, what do you see? Is the thought in your head being truthful or just telling you what you have been told by others?

- What do other people think of you? How do their responses affect how you feel or think about yourself?

- What coping strategy have you adopted if you have been made to feel worthless? If it is the same strategy you use now, how is it helping you? Might it be time to rethink the strategy?

Chapter 3

Relationships with Men

If only I had known then what I know now
The difference it would have made for my furrowed brow
So much time spent wondering what I was doing wrong
When in fact the only thing I'd needed was to be firm and strong

At least with these insights
There is no need for you to fret
Just think and reflect inwards
To make the change instead

Michelle Ensuque

Once upon a time…

Now, don't get me wrong. I adore a good love story, the happy-ever-afters, the furtive glances, the touching of hands, the secret smiles and caresses. Unfortunately, what is missing is that, firstly, true love is hard to find (I can hear a song pinging in my head somewhere), and secondly, it's even harder to maintain. For the majority of women, we are brought up on fairy tales, where the prince meets the princess, he sweeps her off her feet, they kiss and the next minute they are swishing down the aisle, getting married and living happily ever after. Maybe things have moved on a little since I was young, when these books and movies were quite prevalent, although I still see a lot of that in Disney films even now. Thank goodness I had two boys: Matt, the eldest, who can't bear being called Matthew, his given name; and Josh, just over two years younger, who can't bear being called Joshua, his given name, either! We would regularly feast on action movies rather than romance and love's impossible dream – those movies I had feasted on when I was much younger, but I quickly realised that expectation set in movies was far removed from reality. *Mission: Impossible* (which might as well represent my attempts at successful relationships); James Bond; *Fast and Furious* – they were more likely to be my go-to fiction escapism.

You might think that I should devote this chapter to how horrible my partners and ex-husband were and spill the beans on what they said and did. You might consider that reasonable. While it might be tempting to show their less than ideal sides, I'm not going to. You see, this book is about how I reacted to those things that happened, and about the realisation that I managed to overcome a rather shaky start. Admittedly it was through sheer grit and determination, but also through a lot of reflection and work on myself. I say 'shaky', which seems a pathetic adjective given the context, but I can't think of a better one right now as nothing does the situation justice. The pain I had experienced didn't break me. You know the phrase: 'what doesn't break you makes you stronger.' That might have been the case for a while, but for me now I would say that, as well as being more resilient, I had smoothed the rough edges. I understood when enough was enough. I am a much nicer and kinder version of the person that previously existed, including to myself. However, there is no doubt whatsoever that those early years lacked positive male role models – except my grandad, of course, but I was so young when he died. This affected my ability to recognise unkindness or act on it when I did notice it. I put up with poor behaviour towards me, time and time again, because it was 'normal'. I know it's not right to put up with it, but I understand why it's hard to recognise it when it happens and why we stay when really we should leave.

So what had I learned from my childhood? Fundamentally, even as early as twelve or thirteen, I learned I was ugly – the kind that no one wants. I'd also learned this was my fault. I had made myself this way, so I figured I should be able to change it. This view continued right up until I had therapy and neurolinguistic programming (NLP) in my late forties. Now when I look back, it feels as though I wasted so much of my life on something that was not of my making. I certainly don't see myself as ugly now.

I'd also learned that poor behaviour is acceptable; violence is part of our existence; I am powerless; and if I stand up for myself there will be a consequence, and it won't be anything good. I'd learned that emotions can dangle on a knife edge. You have to be adept in working out when the mood changes and when to walk away. I'd learned that conflict meant anger and that marriage was not necessarily a place for happiness.

I was also scared. Of boys. Of sex. Of having babies outside marriage. Fundamentally, I was scared of the reaction of my parents to those things rather than scared of the events themselves. Honestly, sometimes I was scared of my own shadow. I remember once when I was sixteen, travelling home, early afternoon, on a train from Cardiff to Hereford. I used to be a musician, a flautist, and had to travel to Cardiff for flute lessons. As I sat in a compartment in the rickety old train, alone (the train had few passengers), staring out of the window, a young man came in. He sat down and said: "Eh up, darling. You don't remember me, do you? I'm Richard." I was startled and taken off guard. I thought: is it my cousin? I wasn't close to all of my dad's family, but I knew there was a cousin called Richard. Was it a coincidence or had he recognised me? I muttered, "No," but before the word was even out of my mouth, he had come over to sit next to me. I felt uncomfortable. Why couldn't he go away and leave me alone? I stared out of the window, giving perfunctory answers to his questions, but I also snuck a glance every now and then, trying to remember if I had seen him on family photos. After all, it would be a bit rude not to know your own family. As he got more irritating, I moved my hand out slowly to find my bag and flute. I was going to leave and go somewhere else. Luckily, my hand found the leather straps, but I had barely risen from the seat when he leapt into action. I suddenly found myself forced back into the seat with my head in the crook of his arm, in a headlock, facing his lap. My stomach clenched and my head reeled in disbelief. *He can't be doing this on a train in broad daylight, surely? Please God, no.* His other hand was over my mouth. I felt sick. I was sweating. My mind was whirring. *Will the ticket man come past? Is the train due a stop? If my head stays locked like this, will I miss my stop?* I couldn't remember the stops on the way to mine. *Please will someone save me!*

Then, in my head, silence. I knew in that moment I was the only person who could stop this. I rammed my elbow with all my might into his groin. I'd done judo as a kid and figured it was reasonable to use it in this situation. Plus those action movies made it look easy. His body jerked and a kind of 'oof' sound came out of his mouth as his knee came up and his arm released me. Without looking back, I grabbed my stuff, wrenched the sliding door open and fled. I ran up the train and joined another compartment, but this time with a group of people who barely looked up from their newspapers. Luckily, my stop was coming up soon.

I was a mess. My head was in a mess. I could feel the sweat under my armpits and dripping down my back, but outwardly I looked calm. All the time I was thinking, *Don't walk past, don't walk past*, because if he found me he would be angry, and he would probably wait. How would I get off the train? Yet at the same time I didn't know whether I had just elbowed a complete stranger or my cousin in the balls. Had I asked him to do what he did? Had I somehow led him on? Why hadn't I left as soon as he entered? I was a teenager. What did I know? I'd never even kissed a boy! From the moment he entered the compartment, I'd felt like a frightened deer; I was paralysed. All my instincts told me to run, but the 'good girl' in me had stayed put. I did what I was told. To leave for no reason, even if instinct told you otherwise, would have been rude. What I screamed the most in my head was: *why me?*

Once the train drew into Hereford station, I ran off the train as fast as I could and didn't stop until I felt I was safe. There were no shops – just a pub further up on the main street, but it would be closed. All I wanted to do was get to a place that was busy with cars or people; so, running left out of the station, I ran towards the bridge on the main road. For all I knew he might have been watching, waiting for a moment to seek his revenge, and I still had to walk home, which was more than a mile away, so I waited on that bridge just to make sure he hadn't followed me, and then I started the walk home. When I did arrive, I went straight to my room. I didn't tell anyone. It was humiliating. What scared me most was the knowledge that in the coming weeks I had to go to Cardiff again. I just hoped I didn't see him. To repeat those journeys took courage and strength. Then, after a while, just as the memory was fading, a black-and-white photograph was put up in Hereford station. A young man was wanted for sexual assault. He had attacked someone on a train. No doubt it was the same man. The face was exactly the same – even now I can picture the jawline. The incident raced into my mind faster than a greyhound chasing a rabbit, and I felt sick to my stomach. So – it wasn't just me. But I said nothing. Telling people would mean my dad would know, and so no, I'd rather keep it to myself. Part of it was also denial. If I didn't report it, I could bury it, pretend it hadn't happened and crack on with my life. So I buried it where no one could find it, and the next day I woke up and thought: *Today is another day*.

My first boyfriend was a much older man than me, and was someone who worked with me. At the time I met him he was just a few years younger than my dad, and he was the first real man who had shown any interest in me. Perhaps I was attracted to him because, as an only child, I had been surrounded by older males, and honestly I found boys my own age confusing, but in truth he looked much younger than his forty-eight years. This man took the lead and I was used to being obedient. We went out for around eighteen months. I can't remember much about it, maybe because it was another negative thing from my past I chose to delete – in my head, at least. It was fun at first, going to dinner, but – and this was to become a recurring theme in later years – there was no commitment. However, I do remember the end clearly. I was living in some dump in Coventry and he lived around the corner. We had no hoover, so I asked to borrow his. Did he offer to drop it round at mine? No. At that point, did I say 'OK, don't bother then'? No. No, I cycled to his house and shoved the hoover in the basket on the front of the bike. All I needed was a sheet and we could have had a complete re-enactment of *E.T.*! However, while I was clearing up, I realised having to experience the humiliation of cycling home with that hoover in the basket – rather than him offering his help – signalled this relationship was over. When I returned it, I simply said it had sucked up everything like he had sucked out the joy from me, and we were done. He looked relieved, actually, with a slimy smirk stuck on his face. Christ, how I wish I had slapped the hoover across his mouth that day.

Fast-forward a few years and it appears I had gathered some mettle in my armour somehow, but again when it was too late. I was working in London and seeing someone I worked with. I say 'seeing' – I think nowadays it would be 'friends with benefits', but in my case it seemed to be missing the 'friends' bit. Like all princesses, I imagined he would fall in love with me. Instead he fell for a pretty French waitress. We all worked in the same restaurant, and I once spied them in an intense embrace at the back of the building where we took our breaks. I didn't let on that I knew. In fact, I befriended her (yes, he knew) just to annoy him. She was funny, deliciously pretty, sexy in that 'je ne sais quoi' French way, and sweet. Then one day when he was 'seeing' me, I left him, undressed, tied to a bedpost in some second-rate hotel in a rather excitable state. I've no doubt that excitement dissipated pretty quickly afterwards, especially when it became obvious why I was so pissed off. I was also mad because he had taken a watch from me – a birthday gift from Mum – and not returned it, saying he was going to get it repaired. It was probably wrapped around the

Frenchy's dainty wrist. Naturally, the restaurant owner was concerned about how this was all going to pan out, especially when I said, "Well, if he just leaves me alone and returns my watch, I won't need to report him for working here illegally, will I?" The guy in question was Greek, and I suspected he was working without a visa; judging by my boss's reaction, I was probably right. See? Told you I'd learned some skills. Quite chuffed with myself, I was. Needless to say, the watch was not returned, so when he asked how much it was worth, I highly inflated the value. He paid me the money and I bought myself a lovely watch in Hatton Garden. Life was sweet.

So far, no love story. No happy ever after. Not even a sniff. But I'm no quitter and, as if fate was about to come to my aid, I met my first husband at a New Year's Eve party, the night before my thirtieth birthday. I'd gone to a party with a friend and her boyfriend and was drawn to a lovely-shaped pair of arms. Don't laugh! It was clear this man looked after himself, so his bulging biceps and his smile, which showed gleaming white, perfectly straight teeth, piqued my interest. And, ladies and gentlemen, he asked me to dance. Woohoo! OK, now we can play the bride music, right? Well, yes, of course, there was the outrageous clue – 'husband'.

So is this where we have the happy ever after? No. Now, I'm the first to say that if we look back at things and cannot find any happy memories at all, we are deluding ourselves. Even looking at the situation with my parents, we did have some good times, and I hold the view that they did the best they could with the tools they had in the box. OK, they should have bought some new tools, but that's being picky.

We can love people in that moment; we may fall out of love at some point, but that doesn't mean it was all bad. However, if

I had listened to my inner voice when my husband proposed, I would have politely declined. There was a loud *No!* in my head when he said those words, but my lips replied 'yes'. Actually, he proposed in a lovely setting and it was unexpected, but to this day I remember that word appearing in my mind.

Of course, now I've learned to trust it, but then I swatted it away like an annoying fly. I was thirty-one, and while babies were not on my agenda, I was aware of the ticking clock; and with the previous experiences I'd had of men, this didn't seem bad at all. And it wasn't! We laughed during rainy camping holidays in France (honestly, I hate…no, detest camping). We laughed at how the highlight of our excursions was a visit to Carrefour to admire the rows of lettuce and other garden delights. Yes, really. We had a veggie garden, and a green house. We loved creating things from scratch such as home-made sausages. We liked travelling, particularly to India. Hubby had mapped out the route around Rajasthan, which we took by car, chauffeur driven. It wasn't posh or expensive, the iconic Ambassador, but it was a memory, nonetheless. Particularly when someone crashed into us and the driver asked if we could stay somewhere for the night while it was fixed. We looked in disbelief when, the next morning, that same car had been panel beaten within an inch of its life and looked pristine.

OK, I'm struggling now. No, I'm joking. We have two fabulous boys and I wouldn't wish that away. But you get the drift. We had some nice times. Now, equally I could tell you about the negative moments of those holidays or activities, but that is not the point. The point is what I did with or about those negative occurrences. Absolutely nothing. Just like the incident on the train or the abuse at the hands of my parents. It took me a long time to say that word – 'abuse' – and it still makes me cringe. I was the twelve-year-old girl who was told not to speak, to keep my mouth shut, who instead was screaming inside my head and making two white fists under the table. My opinion was not important. Children should be seen and not heard, we were told.

To get out of my ten-year marriage I had an affair, very briefly. I'm not proud and it wasn't intentional. In fact, if anyone had ever suggested I would do such a thing, I would have laughed. I considered myself far too moral. But I did. I'd never do it again, as now I know I have the skills to go about things differently. I also know I can live and enjoy life alone; and, more importantly, my self-esteem isn't shot to oblivion. But this is now, and that was then. It was just weeks into the affair that I spilled the beans to my hubby. I had met someone who made me laugh, and in that moment I no longer felt the same for my husband. Well, for a long time I'm not sure what I had felt. In fact, my self-esteem had eroded away like a dripping tap, so that by the end there was nothing left. As I was clearly such a disappointment, I felt I wouldn't be missed; but nothing prepared me for the emotional roller coaster that ensued.

I had had a vision. I joined the Royal Air Force in 1991 and signed up for sixteen years' service. When I married in 1996, I imagined we would stay married for ever and provide our children, once we had had them, with all the love and support that I had rarely felt in my upbringing. We had spoken of plans to live in America once I had retired from the RAF, with my husband working and me looking after our children; but as the years went by, all I could imagine was an empty feeling wherever we went. I divorced my husband in four months, when my boys were three and five, and also ditched the other guy, in the knowledge that I didn't want him either. He was merely the catalyst that got me moving. I wanted no one.

What I wanted was to be alone. As was my personality, I decided not to look back. It was done. With all my other relationships, I deleted the other party from my life as though they never existed. In truth, I didn't delete my hubby. I couldn't. We had to find a way to smooth the path for our boys. Today we can share a meal together and exchange messages with no nastiness. Life has moved on. But back then, I deleted the good memories in my head and focused on the reason for turning all our lives upside down.

As I was nearing the end of my sixteen years' service, I had to make a decision. Stay in and risk being moved around or being detached for four to six months overseas, or leave the RAF. I couldn't take the chance with the former, unleashing an unstable lifestyle and lack of security on my boys; so I moved house, took project management qualifications and changed jobs, all in the space of a year. It was great for weight loss! For me, stress meant I couldn't taste anything; food tasted like sawdust. Strange now that that was the positive I saw even though, for the first time in many years, I felt free.

I had one more relationship before I met my now-husband and, despite it being eight years long, I have little to say about it. It is the familiar story of me not sticking up for myself, not being honest with myself and not having the guts to end it sooner than I did, so it is not my intention to bore you to tears. Again, we had great times – especially in the early years, when I was happy not to have commitment and to have the space to look after my boys and work, and then on alternate weekends, when the boys were with their dad, enjoy some downtime. However, halfway through the relationship I suffered my breakdown.

Juggling work, children and a part-time partner (so-called because I saw him every other weekend at best) was exhausting. My past had finally caught up with me. My dad had died, my stepmother was focused on getting as much money as possible, and my bank account went down to zero after I had paid for all the funeral costs and paid her off. That added more pressure to my already tenuous existence, and I told no one how I really felt about these financial issues. The only person I spoke to was me in my head.

Once I had crashed, rather spectacularly, to rock bottom, I spent a year recovering. After that, though, my experience made me reflect on where I was at. I could only just look after myself and my boys, so didn't have time to devote to whether I should end the relationship or not. I questioned whether it was me or us. I guess in the end that didn't really matter. In the end that theme of lack of commitment reared its ugly head…I hadn't even talked about marriage! So when I tested it and came up wanting, I gave up.

So here is what I didn't do from the ages of twenty to forty-nine:

- I didn't point out that hurtful remarks hurt me when they were made. I put up with them and hurt inside instead.
- I didn't stand up for my independence. Creating a joint account ended up as a bad idea but I didn't stand up for me, even though I was earning a really good salary.
- I didn't put boundaries in place around acceptable behaviour. In truth I hadn't even heard of boundaries until recent years.
- I thought I was seeing the other person's point of view, but was I? I mean, I wasn't perfect. In the RAF I could fall out of bed to go to work, and yet my hubby had to be yanked

around with me wherever we went. On occasion he drove one and a half hours each way to and from work. I didn't appreciate it. I just accepted it, didn't see the growing resentment, and he never spoke about it.

- When I suffered trauma, I didn't seek help. I've written here about the abuse, but in a later chapter I write about the death of my mum, who took her own life when I was seven months pregnant with my first child. I didn't seek help for that either, bar a brief foray with the psychiatrists in the RAF. I didn't deal with it. Neither did I deal with my childhood. I put both in a box and locked them away.
- When my dad died and unleashed the Pandora's box of emotions I'd kept bottled up for forty-eight years, I didn't deal with it until I was forced to, until I was on my knees.
- I couldn't accept conflict, so, short-term, I chose the easy option – to shut up. In essence, I stewed.

My happy ever after…

Cringe! We met on Match.com. Welcome to dating in the twenty-first century. But the interesting thing about Match is you get to tick boxes for your preferences. I increased the height of the person I was looking for. Well, I am short and all my partners have been short, so I figured I'd change it up a little. Apart from my first partner, I'd always been with younger people, and so I sought out men slightly older than me. After submitting my requirements, Alain came up in first place.

Now, two points. First, in his profile picture he was running, and I don't mean for the bus. He was running with a number on his T-shirt. Shit. I rather hoped he wasn't expecting me to complete a half-marathon. Second, he said he liked camping. FFS! As you are well aware, people, it's my idea of holiday hell. All I could do was wait and see. We couldn't meet each other for two weeks as he was in France, so we chatted on the phone and sent many emails back and forth, so much so that when we finally did meet it certainly didn't feel like the first time. We went for a meal, chatted, a waitress accidentally threw ice-cold water over me when she tripped, but the air was 'hot'.

It turned out he hates camping. He had no idea why he had ticked the box. Yes, he enjoys running but he isn't a slave to it, he just loves keeping fit. In turn, I've since introduced him to other forms of exercise (keep it clean, people), such as David Lloyd classes, weight training and cycling. He found me out, though. Asked why I'd lied: apparently, I'd ticked the box for 'speaks other languages: French'. Well, I wasn't lying. *Je m'appelle Michelle* and *elle a une robe rouge* were very useful phrases. I'd learned French at school, so not an outright lie. Except he was French. Bugger. That was going to be trickier. Anyway, he was my frog – I kissed him and he turned into a prince... Aww. Neither of us had met anyone else on Match and we had both been on the site for only a week, but after our meeting we both cancelled our membership!

Alain doesn't just leave it to me to make sure our relationship is enjoyable. He also comes up with ideas and is keen to learn from mistakes he might have made in the past too. One of his best ideas ever was his suggestion of 'review meetings'. We were both project managers. We both held monthly meetings to assess our progress and identify any risks. "Why don't we do that in our life together?" he asked. What an awesome idea! We had actually had our first falling out. We – meaning *I* – had been planning to go away with the boys for a rugby tour weekend early in our relationship.

Now, there are a few things I detest aside from camping,

and one is being in a static home, in the arsehole of nowhere, in the cold, with people I don't know well, freezing on the side of a rugby pitch. So, for me, having Alain with me would have been a saving grace. An opportunity to still enjoy myself instead of getting through it with gritted teeth. Alain had said he would come, so I got on with the organising, but as the date loomed closer I felt something was up, and asked if he still wanted to come. The answer was 'no'. I got it. Why would he, as a six-foot bloke, want to spend a weekend in a glorified caravan with his feet dangling over the edge of a teeny-tiny bed and the rain howling on the windows? Why would he want to stand on the sidelines in the cold to support two kids he didn't really know and a woman he knew only a bit better? But I was disappointed. Not in his choice, but that he had said nothing. We were days away from going and I now had to face going, once again, alone. I adopted my usual approach with the boys of taking the mick out of the situation and drinking copious amounts of red wine. Well, it was a rugby weekend.

After that weekend, Alain and I met for dinner, and of course I ensured I dressed like a sex siren, although that was most definitely not on the menu, and we discussed the issue at great length. That was when the review meetings made their entrance. We both agreed that going out for dinner somewhere neutral once every four to six weeks, just to 'check in' on our relationship, was necessary. The review meetings provided a safe place where we could bring up areas of concern and identify things that were going well. It was not overshadowed by high emotion, it was simply a lovely thing to do. But it felt useful. We had action plans that we would manage and report back on at the next session. Nowadays our conversations are more fluid. We don't need a 'review' meeting as such to bring up any issues, but we still do them. It was, and is, undoubtedly one of the best ways we can express ourselves to each other and learn about each other.

The thing I learned most is that to find the perfect person for me, I had to be me. Not what I thought the other person wanted me to be. When I stripped all that away, looked at my past, whom I had pleased, whom and what I had put up with, I felt angry. Angry for my lost childhood. Angry for mostly having to cope alone. Angry at people taking advantage of my good nature and kindness. Angry at life always seeming so fucking hard. But being angry got me to a different place…

The things I did do and have done:

- I set out to Alain two things I detested – smoking and unkindness. In fact, I said: "If you do something unkind, I will tell you immediately, I won't stew." I have been true to my word ever since. He has said: "While it isn't nice to hear sometimes, at least I know what the issue is, and I can deal with it."
- I asked him loads of questions that were directly related to finding out how he operated, as a person and in relationships, and I delved deeper if I thought there was more to it. To his credit, he did the same in return.
- I don't pretend to like something I don't, just to please him. However, I do try things I know he likes, and we don't just do things that I alone enjoy.
- I've used my NLP training to deal with tricky situations and I don't hide or shy away from conflict, although to be fair there has been very little during our seven years. Ask me in ten years when I've lodged an axe in his head (*joke!*).
- I've stood up for myself where others are blatantly in the wrong.
- I try to listen. I have a tendency to jump in, to want to find

solutions – sometimes I am more man (in my experience) than woman in that respect. I have learned to sit and wait.
- I've tried to see things truly from his point of view. I haven't always got it right, but I like to think I am much better at it.

A friend asked me once how I knew Alain was the right one. I said: "Because he takes up no space in my head. I don't have to wonder if he loves me, I just know he does. I don't have to think about why he's behaving in such a way or try to work out what he is thinking, because we communicate openly with each other. My brain is simply at peace." And here we are, happily married, living in France – where, bizarrely, my ex-husband also lives with his new partner. So happy-ever-afters do exist, but bloody hell, no one wrote all that in-between stuff in the 'once upon a time' books, did they?

What might this mean for you?

- What behaviours might you be adopting that allow others to continue to treat you badly?

- What behaviours are you willing to accept from others and why?

- What are your values? Do they correspond with those of your partner?

- On a scale of one to ten (one being 'I never do' and ten being 'always'), how much do you stand up for what you believe in with a partner? If the score is low, what stops you doing that and what might help you improve on that score?

- If you are fearful of standing up for yourself, or of leaving a partner, what consequences do you believe will occur as a result? What could you do to allay those fears?

- If you find yourself dwelling on how others are behaving towards you and worrying about what they will do next, what would you be focusing on instead if you weren't doing that?

Chapter 4

Relationship with Food

Do I not destroy my enemies when I make them my friends?
Unknown

What on earth does my relationship with food have to do with those early years and my eventual depression? Well, as with a good suspense thriller, bear with me until the end, when all will become clear.

I cannot remember a time, until recently, when food was ever my friend. Even now and then we occasionally do a little dance when we throw caution to the wind before, once again, we enter the ring to fight. In those moments I rarely feel victorious, just battle-worn and scarred. Up until the age of about twelve or thirteen, though, I don't remember food being an issue at all. In fact, I have barely any memories about food, including, as I've mentioned, eating at Grandad's. Food, it appears, was a complete non-event. However, I do remember my mum making me sit at the table and eat pork fat when I was seven or eight. Not the crispy, salty, luscious kind (you can feel the fat sliding down your throat to your hips, but who cared, it was bliss); no, the soggy, wobbly blancmange, subcutaneous fat left over from the Sunday roast. I have no idea why. Who actually eats that stuff? What was the lesson (other than control) about being made to eat it? It was vile, and I didn't see anyone else putting it in their mouths. In the end I had to hide it. It kept coming out for every meal, and I was starting to get hungry because I wasn't allowed to eat anything else until I had gobbled it up like some strange delicacy. When it came out for the second day at breakfast time, I took my chance. My mum turned around at a knock on the door and I secreted it into my pocket. Perhaps, at that moment, I felt victorious. It wasn't the only time I was forced to eat something. Liver with the blood still oozing from it was another, but pork fat was definitely the worst.

I was podgy when I was younger. No two ways about it. I think, left to my own devices, though, I could have turned out normal – 'normal' being slim, less of a disappointment and without the constant noise in my head around being fat and the (negative) association with food. I was never going to be tall, having been short-changed (pun intended) in that area, but a growth spurt and normal eating habits, such as being allowed to leave food on the plate without being shouted at, or not being forced to follow strict diets, would probably have been enough – although this wasn't a house where you were left to your own devices. You did what you were told and you spoke when you were spoken to. You ate what you were given and you weren't allowed to leave anything on your plate. Now, I don't think these were unusual circumstances. Parents raised in the war years were very aware of rationing and grateful for plentiful food. Therefore, waste was not permitted. I understood that, and despite not liking certain foods, I ate them nonetheless. What I hated was having everything put on my plate for me, my

portions decided for me, the meals exactly the same every week:
- Monday: Cold meat from leftover roast and veg; stewed fruit
- Tuesday: Curry, made from leftover roast; stewed fruit
- Wednesday: Sausages and veg with gravy; stewed fruit
- Thursday: Omelette and the occasional cooked custard by mistake, poured over our vegetables; stewed fruit (minus the custard)
- Friday: Fish (always fish on a Friday) with veg; stewed fruit
- Saturday: Sandwiches or toast all day (this was Mum's day off cooking)
- Sunday: Roast; probably a crumble – with stewed fruit, of course.

Never a variation, unless we went out to the pub – which they did quite a bit with their friends later on, to be fair – or under extreme circumstances. My dad's company once went on strike, and this was worrying: it appeared to put our ability to buy sausages for the Wednesday night meal in serious peril. Yet somehow we managed to scrape enough money together. Later on in life I vowed never to force my kids to eat the food I served up, never pressure them to eat what they didn't want (I just asked them to consider that tastes change and to keep trying different things), and I never made the same meal the same day each week.

The dullness that existed in our culinary experiences at my house was occasionally interspersed with some baking, which always happened on Thursdays. I was never allowed to assist, for fear of making a mess. My mum was not blessed in the baking department, bless her; some things turned out well, and she made a mean giggle cake (so-called because it split its sides in the oven, apparently), but if it wasn't for the inch-thick wood on the kitchen table, I swear her sponges would have slipped through like a sharp knife through soft butter. But Christmas cakes were always decorated, meals were always provided for us and, God love her, she did her best.

My dad's view on food, though, was very different. "Eat faster, you aren't leaving the table until you've finished your plate," he'd bark. To this day I have to force myself to slow down my eating because otherwise I'd hoover my food before anyone had barely started, for fear of any punishment if I ate too slowly. Being constantly told I was fat and yet being told to eat all my food was a bit of a surreal environment to be in. Taken to the doctor's for appetite-reducing tablets, constantly weighed and monitored, to be told I was a disappointment – all of this was psychological torture. Even when I have been slim, I have never seen myself as such. I have never thought of myself as pretty, and hated – still sometimes hate – looking at photos of myself.

Meals weren't the battleground with my parents; life was. But there was clearly only one reason I could be overweight, I thought, and that was because of food. So my relationship with it became skewed. I ended up bingeing on food and then tried to hide it. I did it because I felt I could, even though it was in secret. Perhaps it was the only thing I had control over. In a funny way, it felt like a game. The irony, in that those actions ended up with me being even bigger, was not lost on me. Realising that their approach wasn't getting anywhere, my parents started operating in stealth mode and enlisted the aid of my cousin to help me lose weight. She was lovely about it and took me out for a meal in a pub. It was like the Last Supper. I felt like I'd eaten my last chip. What my parents didn't understand was that they controlled what I ate, at least until about fourteen or fifteen, when I had my own part-time job and had some money to spend on sweets and other things. If I was eating what they gave me, didn't they have a part to play in this? Why was it my fault and why was it such a fucking problem? The other irony was that whatever problem my parents, or more particularly my dad, had with the way I looked, this seemed to translate to partners too. It was almost as if they had colluded and discussed my disgustingness and how they needed to get me to help myself. Clearly this was for my own benefit. Constant remarks about the size of my stomach (such as "It's a pity about the mother of all bellies"), what I was dressed in, what I looked like and whether I had gained a few pounds were all I heard for about forty years. If they weren't saying it with their mouths, they were with their expressions. It didn't matter, of course, whether I had had a new baby or if I was unhappy; even when I did lose weight, no one ever said anything positive. It was as though it had been expected, so if I did lose weight, good – I should have done!

I did have some success – for me, at least. I followed 1,000-calorie-a-day diets and lost weight quickly over a few weeks. I was ecstatic. It felt very easy; I didn't have to follow a diet for long and the results were evident. I did 1,200 another time, with the occasional treat, and lost the weight I wanted over six weeks. But it got to the stage where I could tell you the calorie content of a cup of tea, a biscuit, a snack, a meal, without even needing to look it up. I was tethered to the calorie counter like a dog on a leash. I never followed a calorie-restricted diet after that. Actually, I lie – I tried in my fifties and the scale registered no change in two weeks. That felt weird when I'd previously been successful, but age, menopause, stress and probably insulin resistance were all factors.

My weight and issues around food contributed to my

eventual depression. I had no sense of self-worth. I felt physically sick when I looked in the mirror, so I tried not to look. When I did, I would examine from all angles, in clothes and out of them. I would pinch my fat and constantly talk to myself about how I needed to do something about it. I would weigh myself constantly and berate myself if I had put on a pound or two. When I got up in the morning, how I felt about what I weighed that morning could negatively impact my mood all day. I looked miserable, literally, and could hardly bear to speak to anyone. The simple act of eating seemed to cause my stomach to distend. I could wear something in the morning and be unable to wear the same thing at night. At certain times of the month, my belly would bloat to such an extent that it looked like I was pregnant. Getting into clothes was a challenge. In the end I visited a doctor because it was psychologically unbearable, and – thank goodness – he said: "If you were my daughter, I'd suggest going on the pill." I could have kissed him there and then for trying to support me and it did actually alleviate the cyclical monthly bloating.

Other than that, I've tried every diet under the sun: blood type; calorie-controlled; low-carb diets such as keto and Atkins; and low-fat, promoted by Rosemary Conley and others (images of leotards and leg warmers spring to mind). I tried the India diet – incredibly successful. Basically, visiting India for three weeks and spending two of them fastened to a toilet, resulting in eight pounds lost in two weeks. Results: ten out of ten. Approach: zero.

I now wonder whether my constant dieting and pressure to exercise most days has, in some capacity, contributed to current health issues. I will never know. We now know that 'low-fat' doesn't necessarily mean healthy, especially when we consider the fact that the food industry has made billions through its sales of 'low-fat' products, where fat has been replaced by sugar to enhance their taste. Cutting out major food groups isn't a good idea either, unless there is a good medical reason.

Some of this research is fascinating and shows how weight is a much more complex issue than was first thought. I've listened to podcasts on this subject and wondered how people operated internally and why everyone was different. Why were some people certain shapes and others different? I knew that people's hormones were not all the same and that not all people function the same way. Take my parents, for example, who were both diabetics – my mum type 1 and my dad type 2. I myself had gestational diabetes during my second pregnancy, so I wondered: if that is the case for hormones (and there are others more closely related to hunger and satiety), what if some of us just process food in a different way? What if our hormones aren't at the optimal level? What if I, for example, was predisposed to insulin resistance, which contributed to my issues? This wasn't even a topic of conversation when I was young, and hadn't existed as a 'thing' until recent years. But when I look back at what we ate when I was a kid, sure, it was healthy. We used vegetables from our garden and fruit from hedgerows, and all our meals were made from scratch. However, every morning was white toast with jam, or cereals; lunch was white bread sandwiches. Pasta and rice were white. Saturdays were white bread at every meal. Sunday evening was crumpets. Doesn't sound a good recipe for diabetics or anyone else predisposed to the effects of the white refined stuff.

Podcasts I listened to talked about how the calorie in isolation is not the entire answer. It's not as simple as calories in versus calories out, and the way it was even determined was a little one-dimensional and simplistic. There is also the role of the microbiome, the definition of 'set point theory', and how neurological inflammation can affect body weight. That was particularly interesting to me, in limbo with an undiagnosed neurological condition: "Possibly MS," said the consultant, with no advance warning. Great, thanks for that potentially life-changing diagnosis! Yet others talked about how emotion and behaviour change are linked and why healing trauma can improve your health and thus your weight loss – or, indeed, gain. Some of those weren't surprising but were interesting nonetheless.

After listening to all of this information, it reaffirmed my thought: what if it wasn't me after all? What if it was a mix of the way I was made, acute childhood trauma (plus the associated fear I had lived with most days) and a lack of information and guidance, other than appetite suppressant tablets and strict diets? We tend to shame 'fat' people for not having enough intelligence or safe control. Yet we don't view other diseases in the same way. If someone has cancer, we don't look at them and think 'well, you've brought that on yourself' – with, perhaps, the exception of smoking. Generally we treat them with compassion and understanding. Compassion and understanding were not things I had ever experienced. I had been made to feel shameful for all those years – made to feel that I was a failure, weak for not being able to resist food. That somehow I had a character flaw and had done this to myself; ironically, the shame of that had perpetuated further overeating, so in fact I did end up doing that to myself. Throughout all of those years, I'd been starving myself of nutrients and struggling to create a perfect me – something that just wasn't possible, because I doubt I would have recognised perfection even if I saw it with my own eyes.

You could say I was a food addict. I would think about food all the time, especially if I was dieting. Remember that calorie leash? If I had eaten supper, I would think of breakfast, and thoughts of breakfast would turn to lunch, and so on. I had to stop calorie-counting and threw out my weighing scales to give my head, never mind my body, a break. It was hard, though. I had memorised so many calories I still processed them in my head when I ate or drank. It took a few years to stop that.

One of the most interesting aspects (I say 'interesting' because I have no idea what drove me) was my ability to continue eating even though I had just had a meal. I knew I wasn't eating because I was hungry. Really I was eating because I loved the taste. As each spoon or fork went into my mouth, I'd move the contents around, savouring the taste before it was quickly dispatched to my stomach. Sometimes I'd think, *Bugger, if I swallow it, it will make me fat*, so sometimes I wouldn't swallow. Sometimes I'd spit it out, having retrieved the taste I wanted – that way it was taste minus calories. You can tell I thought about this a lot. For example, take risotto. If I make a risotto and put a decent portion on my plate, I can't not go back and eat it out of the pan if there are leftovers, even if it's cold. I can do the same with stews and other cooked food and usually things that would make people's stomachs squirm. Not mine. Probably because I ate cold leftover food in secret. Warming it up meant I might be found out. It gave me a momentary sense of pleasure followed by hours' worth of guilt. I used to think I didn't have a problem. People ate whole packets of biscuits, apparently, and I could eat one or two and leave the rest, so I was OK, right? Having a few forkfuls of cold cooked food wasn't a big deal in comparison, or so I told myself.

I remember dinner at someone's house once, and a group

of women were talking about diets and issues with food, and I joined in the chat. One woman quite loudly snorted: "I don't think you've got too much to worry about, dear." From a certain perspective I should have been gratified that she thought like that – that my appearance was everything they aspired to achieve – slim and fit. I was in the RAF and exercised every day. At that point I was indeed slim and wearing a figure-hugging, short, black off-the-shoulder velvet dress (events on the officers' patch, darling, even at people's houses, were posh). From another perspective I wanted to scream: "You don't understand – I feel fat all the time! I think about food all the time – what to eat, what not to eat, what impact it will have on me. It drives me mad and I want it to stop." Of course, I didn't say any such thing – I just smiled, didn't really know what to say, and let them carry on the conversation. Fundamentally, I realised, I just wanted to be included – be part of their gang – but I wasn't.

It was as though food was a constant companion, but one of those whiny ones that kept complaining, droning on and on in my ear from dawn until dusk. It had become intertwined in me: a constant subconscious and sometimes conscious thought, like breathing. And like breathing, I couldn't stop it.

I was a food addict. Physician Gabor Maté's views on this subject are interesting. He considers addiction as not a choice, and it isn't confined to taking drugs or illicit substances. His belief is it can affect a lot of us in many ways (in fact, he says 'all of us', but I don't like generalisations), including gambling, alcohol, food, sugar, shopping, sex or anything else. The issue is not in our genes but in our childhoods. Addiction is a way to escape our pain. In an article in California Healthline (January 2019) he said: "All addictions — alcohol or drugs, sex addiction or internet addiction, gambling or shopping — are attempts to regulate our internal emotional states because we're not comfortable, and the discomfort originates in childhood. For me, there's no distinction except in degree between one addiction and another: same brain circuits, same emotional dynamics, same pain and same behaviors of furtiveness, denial and lying."

That really struck a chord for me. I didn't choose to be addicted to food. It was made the most important part of my world by others, and for all the wrong reasons.

Then there was the constant exercising. Luckily the RAF was a place where we could exercise in our lunch hour with no one raising an eyelid. We had to be fit, end of. I would sometimes exercise twice a day. I'd often do the same thing while strictly monitoring what I ate. That is no bad thing, but long-term it becomes all-consuming. In my thirties, I was sprinting in the gym when I felt what can only be described as a sizzle in my lower back. Doesn't feel good, I thought. I was right. By the end of the day I was bent over, and was diagnosed with a slipped disc. I was lucky. I was referred to a top physiotherapist at the Nuffield Hospital in Oxford, who loved his research. By the time I saw him I had already seen a surgeon, who was poised, scalpel in hand, ready to insert a rod into my spine to preserve its stability. Instead, the physiotherapist told me: "You are fitter than the majority of people I see. I think you can overcome this by doing simple exercises that work on the deep internal muscles of the pelvic girdle, and stop running." Woah. Back up. Stop running? Are you kidding me? I will end up looking like Jabba the Hutt in no time!

Initially I ignored him, but I'd pay for the exercise I did do later. Pain, all down my leg and in my buttock. So I stopped, but I was terrified the weight would creep back on. Actually, I lost weight. That was such a surprise and vaguely ironic, but it was an incentive to concentrate on what he told me to do – and he was right. I did those exercises for a year and didn't run during that time. I never did have the surgery, and apart from the odd back issue since, my discs have not been a cause for concern. Now I do the right exercises to maintain my back muscles.

I had tried to tackle things head on when I was in my forties. I figured I should confront my dad and talk to him about the things that had happened when I was young. I thought this might be liberating in some way. I was nervous, though, about raising this topic; but literally as I was about to open my mouth, dressed in a bikini, sitting on his terrace in his house in Spain, he said: "You've got a gut on you, haven't you?" I was shocked. I was forty-three or forty-four, weighed roughly nine stone five (just over 60 kilos) and I was fit, most definitely not fat. Yet my stomach still appeared to be the main topic of conversation. I grew a pair of balls that day, because that comment had played right into my hands and I was angry.

"Why do you have to do that?" I asked.

"Do what?"

"Criticise. Why can't you just be proud of me the way I am?"

His response absolutely floored me. "I've only been proud of you once, and that was when you graduated from the Royal Air Force."

Wow. Ladies and gentlemen. There you have it. Once in forty-three years I amounted to something worthy of pride. You could have forgiven me for leaving there and then, but I pushed. "Once in forty-three years? That's it? OK, so why did you treat me like you did when I was young, then?"

"What do you mean?" he asked.

"The hitting, the beatings, the psychological trauma. That, Dad."

His answer: "I don't know what you mean. You obviously have an overactive imagination."

Is there a sound associated with being floored? If you are floored more than once, is the sound magnified? I knew this was a useless conversation. Any hopes or thoughts I'd had about him begging forgiveness, apologising, giving me a hug, were swiped away in a swift backhand. I was back to being twelve, where of course I was in the wrong. I was also angry, but strangely it did feel like a weight had been lifted from my shoulders. I knew what had happened when I was younger. Despite no one surviving to attest to my experiences, I knew. With no brothers or sisters, there was no one else to turn to, but I was no liar. Yet both of my parents seemed able to pull the blinds down on that area of our lives. To the outside world they were a normal couple. Smiling, talking, my dad was cracking jokes. To me they were manipulative, unkind, cold, vicious and disrespectful too much of the time. I didn't feel safe with them, but also knew nothing else. I really couldn't believe I was from the same mould as these people; in essence their actions directly resulted in me wasting over half my life with a shocking body image and low self-esteem, worrying about something that should have been enjoyed rather than abhorred.

Perhaps for my dad it was too shameful to admit. Perhaps like my mum, who went around the house closing the windows so that our neighbours couldn't hear my screams, he too didn't want to shine the spotlight on his poor parenting skills. Perhaps, though, he really did believe that I had deserved that treatment – that he had done no wrong and that it was simply something I should have just accepted with no complaint. Well, there is a line, people, and for me that line had been crossed.

I finally decided to tackle my issue with food properly in my fifties. Why I had waited for so long I had no idea. In truth, I'd had other things on my mind. I'd had therapy for other issues, but I think I thought this could never be 'fixed'. However, I did have a breakthrough when I tried hypnotherapy. I had tried NLP and it hadn't changed much. I don't see NLP as a panacea to world peace. It's why I advocate people trying anything that works for them and to keep trying other methods if something doesn't work first time. I'd been recommended a lady named Melanie Gillespie, now a business coach but formerly a hypnotherapist. I was heartened, when I sat down in front of her, to hear her using the same approach I do when talking to clients. I thought she would put me into some kind of trance and I wouldn't be able to control anything. She made me feel comfortable – that I could trust the process and relax. I remember one question in particular: "If you weren't eating in secret, what would you be doing instead?" My response was instant: "If I was eating and someone came downstairs or into the room, I would be able to continue eating and not care." Doesn't sound much, does it? Sounds simple. But what I realised was that I did eat in secret, a lot, and I did so in fear that someone would find me eating and shout at me, or worse. The realisation that I was still that child, constantly on the lookout for danger. That eating was bad, so it had to be done in secret.

Anyone who has seen me eat, out in public or at their home, would never know. Sure, if you could leap into my head and watch the chaos, as I took each bite, that bounced from fear to joy, back to fear, to worry, to disgust and self-loathing, then you might have known. Thank goodness you can't, as you might worry about my sanity! I'd panic about having to go out for a meal, and would feel relief when those plans were cancelled so that I could control what went into my mouth. That was no way to live.

After the hypnotherapy I went home, and a few days later I tested my new approach. Though, of course, it wasn't a conscious thought – until I was doing it. I stood in the kitchen, hand in the drawer, about to snaffle a handful of crisps when I heard my younger son walk down the stairs. Now, prepare yourself for something extraordinary. I – carried – on – eating! For any of you who don't have an eating problem (and thank goodness if you do not), that won't seem such a revelation. But for me? It was liberating. And…guess what? As I continued to eat and chat to Josh (not with my mouth full you understand – manners…) I realised nothing had happened. No shouting had occurred. The world hadn't ended, the sky hadn't fallen in. There was just me, my son and a handful of crisps in the setting of everyday life.

I realised my experiences from my childhood, many of which focused on my appearance and which had continued in my relationships, had totally messed up my ability to see myself as anything but fat and ugly. I felt like I was in a prison of my own mind. That particular day I'd been let out on parole, to explore normal life outside the prison, to taste freedom. Little by little I would taste more days of freedom, more days on parole to explore the outside world. My new normal.

NLP might not have cured me of my issues with food, but it helped me become curious. I was like a sponge. I started reading more, listening to more podcasts, reading books and conducting research. It cemented my view that therapy is not 'one size fits all'.

And now?

Where am I? Broadly, I am content. The prison exists, but I am not in it as a life resident. I have the key to unlock the door. I can now look in a mirror and be happy with the way I look – most of the time. I hardly think about food in between meals, apart from seeing how creative I can get or taking inspiration from others. I can accept I don't like all photos of myself, and prefer to adopt the attitude of 'they didn't catch my best side, darling', but some I truly love.

I have reframed food into something to be curious about and understand how it can help my body stay healthy. 'Reframing' is simply a term we use in NLP to redefine something in a more positive way. For example, my issue around food was the fact it made me fat. So I reframed it as a challenge instead and thought about how I could use food to nourish and benefit me and maintain a healthy body and mind. The initial way I saw food was as a problem, and a pretty weighty one…sorry, couldn't resist a joke. But seeing it as a challenge helped me view it as a possible solution, a much more positive perspective. There are all sorts of ways NLP can be used for all sorts of problems, but this is how it has helped me.

I enjoy food. I love the thought of giving my body a fighting chance to be happy – that makes me smile. A few things have enabled me to see food as a positive. There has been a growing trend of understanding how food helps us stay healthy and, in some cases, fight disease – from plant-based studies and their benefits to the timing of when we eat, such as the circadian rhythm and practices such as fasting.

You might think these are just other obsessions I have with food or are ways of controlling what I eat, but you'd be wrong. Being curious about different practices gives me ideas about how I can help myself stay healthy. In the western world, many of us have access to food twenty-four-seven. We don't have to find it like in our hunter-gatherer days. We can get it delivered straight to our door. We don't have to labour on the land like we used to, and technology has delivered the holy grail of an easy life, with inventions such as smart apps to turn appliances on and off, appliances to wash and dry clothes – I'm still hoping someone invents an automatic ironing device, but you get my drift. Don't get me wrong, these are fantastic inventions, but we are a diseased nation. On top of obesity and poor nutrition we have escalating numbers of people with diabetes and other autoimmune diseases. Pills are dished out like Smarties, with no real understanding of what other effects they might be having on our complex systems. When we suffer those effects, we are dished out more pills to treat those. I am not dissing western medicine. Far from it. What I am doing is considering if other approaches could help or be used alongside mainstream practices and reduce the medications required. There is no doubt that alternative medicine has come a long way, but I fear we have a way to go. Of course, there is the multibillion-dollar pharmaceutical industry, but that is a whole other topic.

I love the circadian approach, which links heavily to intermittent fasting. Remember the slogan 'breakfast is the most important meal of the day'? Our universal idea of breakfast didn't really become a 'thing' until the early nineteenth century, when office working became more prevalent or people who were required to come to work early and carry out physically demanding jobs were encouraged to eat before they arrived.

It has been documented that fasting overnight (not eating or drinking anything other than water) can not only help regulate weight control but can also have other health benefits; reduction of inflammation, lowering of blood sugars, the ability of our bodies to regenerate, or remove unwanted or old cells during development, eliminating potentially cancerous and virus-infected cells, and maintain balance in the body. Woah! How cool is that?

Because of my own health issues, I wanted to see if I could alleviate some symptoms through food. Having visited a Thalasso Spa in Roscoff in 2019, I went to a lecture on 'leaky gut' syndrome. I was not a newcomer to this, but Dr Marchaland's presentation intrigued me. It had first come up in my experiences with a kinesiologist, to whom I had taken my son to see if we could improve his eczema symptoms. Dr Marchaland explained that fasting had been trialled with people with severe arthritis and other inflammatory diseases. The results showed that fasting lowered blood glucose levels and significantly reduced inflammation.

I have since read articles on the National Library of Medicine online site which explain how fasting can reduce glucose and may provide a hostile environment to cancer cells, either in prevention or treatment. I've also read that fasting is sometimes used as a therapy in neurological disease, epilepsy, diabetes, MS and so much more, and more information is given to us all the time. This research might be challenged or superseded, but right now, armed with this information, it is enabling me to make some decisions and almost experiment with how my body feels as a result.

Of course, as with everything, there is context and nuance. I know people who have lung cancer and had healthy lifestyles and never smoked. I get that. But I like to believe I have the capacity to help myself after years of depriving myself, which was what got me into this position in the first place. I find fasting easier than other methods I have tried. Plus it's made me realise how much I was absent-mindedly stuffing food into my face while watching TV or wandering in and out of the kitchen, meaning that I was often only going without food for six to eight hours overnight. I've never been a fan of breakfast anyway. I'd eat it – usually those disgusting Corn Flakes – and (less likely after a full English) be hungry two hours later. More importantly, I've learned that a little bit of what you fancy does you good. I like that; nothing is off limits.

I also now follow the Ayurvedic way of eating, and that is very much focused on nourishment and maintaining a healthy body. In fact, the whole Ayurvedic approach is one of calm and of connecting good digestion with the brain and nervous system. Why am I telling you this? Because you have a choice and deserve to be informed. I don't have all the research results. I don't know what works, what doesn't and who it might work for. All I know is my early attitude to food contributed to my mental well-being and possibly my physical well-being too. However, food can also have a positive impact on our lives. I would love for you to be curious. And not just with food but with whatever issues you have faced. Ask questions. Seek answers. Take some control – for you. Don't just put up with issues or suffer because you think that is just the way you are or you don't deserve anything better. You are worth a lot more than that. If you recognise you have a problem, seek therapy – whatever works for you. Remember, if one type doesn't work, try another.

The final thing that has changed for me is being with a man who loves me for who I am, who constantly tells me he thinks I'm beautiful, who doesn't criticise me for having a food baby after a big meal or poke fun of my wobbly bits. He said: "I don't know why you worry so much. Out of the two of us I am more likely to have weight issues than you." This might be a fair comment. He is French, and his relationship with cheese is like his relationship with me: he cannot imagine living without it. Having the freedom to just be me, not to try to be another version of me to keep someone else happy, to have the notion that food is to be enjoyed and used to fuel and nourish, is a lovely place to be. Liberating.

This has made me realise that, like the complexities of our bodies in processing food, our minds are as complex and unique. We are all different. We all have different experiences, backgrounds, culture, needs. Yours won't be the same as mine. As with our relationship with food, we are exposed to external factors. Think of things like fat and gluten: the Darth Vaders of the food industry when suddenly we are told they are 'bad' for us. They aren't all bad for all of us, but we believe it. We go into overdrive. We immediately stop eating them and find ourselves looking at the tube of toothpaste, nodding 'good, it's gluten-free'. In reality, many products don't even get to meet gluten in the production line where they are made. Well, it's the same with our experiences. Our minds go into overdrive. We can be told we are a failure and in one nanosecond we believe it. We only need to be told once, and especially when we are children. Children are fabulous at being imaginative; they can create something out of nothing. So imagine giving them one word, be it ugly, fat, stupid, thick, useless. Imagine what story they can create with that and how real it will become, defining the essence of their being. But it is just a story. Once we realise that, we can create a different one to take its place.

I feel sadness as I look back over those 'wasted' years of my youth, when there was nothing remotely wrong with me. Where, if I had just been left alone, I would probably have been just fine. If you had asked me to state my self-belief in a sentence, I would have simply said: "I am fat." That was all I felt and saw. I feel the torment of all those years and the impossible achievement of perfection. One time I was looking back through photos of my childhood, I saw a photo of a slender girl at fourteen in a red swimming costume on a beach on the Isle of Wight and asked my mum who it was. "It's you!" she said. In my head I was completely taken aback. "That was me? Well, where was Fatty, then?" At least reframing food to friend from foe serves a better purpose than something to be controlled. Now at least it can be enjoyed instead.

What might this mean for you?

- What does food mean to you?

- How much time does dieting, or thinking of food, take up in your head?

- Thinking back to the 'Mirror, mirror on the wall' chapter, how do you see yourself? Is this fact or a story you have been told and continue to tell yourself?

- If you were to reframe how you thought about food, how might you think about it instead?

- What actions could you undertake to help break the dieting/bingeing cycle? Where could you seek help from?

Chapter 5

Left, Right, Left, Right, Attennnnnntion!

Graduating from 134R Squadron on 7 November 1991 was one of the proudest moments of my life. In typical style (I always seemed to have to do everything the hard way), I graduated as part of Recourse Squadron, having completed twelve weeks of training on top of the original sixteen weeks. Those extra twelve weeks were the making of me. They helped me prepare for what was a major life change.

I'd waited two years to join; previously, although I'd succeeded in getting through the three gruelling days of tests, physical and mental, those assessing me said that I had only shown skills in the music industry, and as I wasn't joining the RAF band they wanted evidence I could do other things. So I gave up music and went into the catering industry instead for two years before reapplying. If you put your mind to it, you can achieve what you want. I was no quitter, and this trait appeared to stand me in good stead.

I remember some of the training sessions. The physical ones that made us physically sick – usually running or undertaking circuit sessions straight after breakfast or lunch. Those were never going to end in anything but heaving for me. The psychological ones that required enormous courage to face our fears, whether they were water-based or land-based activities. For me it was heights. I get excruciating vertigo, and having to master the assault course, the top diving board or an arête on top of a Munro in bonnie Scotland took every ounce of my courage and humour. I learned that what was deemed simple by one person was not by another, and this defines the essence of teamwork. We don't all have the same skill sets, and we can offset our weaknesses with the strengths of others. The military enabled that, and it really is the only place where I have seen teamwork work – because it had to. Lives depend on it.

The lecture theatre at RAF Cranwell was warm and cosy, decked with seating guaranteed to send us nodding off in our sleep-deprived state. The punishment was press-ups, to "increase oxygen intake". The practice interviews were numerous, where we would have to interview our subordinates on being late, unacceptable behaviour, running out of money or, in my case, someone suffering from body odour. I remember guffawing. *Why would I need to do that?* I thought. Funny old thing; I had to do that for real during my first tour.

Military training was fantastic. Yes, it was hard, gruelling – physically and mentally – but rewarding. I felt elated, as though I'd come home. While I'd never thought of joining the military until a friend of mine came back home with brochures one day (oddly, I got in and he didn't), the routine, discipline and 'work hard' mantra matched my background perfectly. There were ready-made friends who were my work colleagues, with plentiful social gatherings organised for us. RAF bases were like mini-towns, equipped with gyms, shops, medical and dental centres, and housing. I loved it. For the most part. I was not shy of hard work. I was used to it. I'd worked since I was fourteen. I never treated my RAF work like a nine-to-five job, because it wasn't. You had duties to perform, even at weekends. I've had to deliver news at two in the morning, dressed in my No1 uniform (parade dress), that someone's husband had died. You don't forget those moments. The tears, the screaming. You can't sleep after giving that kind of news to someone. I wondered, every time I had to go on call after that, what might happen. You lived in fear of the phone call about serving overseas, because going to potential war zones meant a huge change to routine. Yet at the same time you accepted it, because this was what you joined up to do. Don't let anyone tell you they loved it wholeheartedly. Most people I spoke to were bricking themselves, even if it held an air of anticipation and excitement.

Then there was the NBC (nuclear, biological and chemical) warfare training. There was nothing salubrious about that. Sweating like a stuck pig in (apparently) NBC-proof clothes, equipped with gas mask and gloves, was not my idea of 'dress up', darling. I'm more of a floaty skirt and stilettos kind of girl. And how the fuck do you go to the loo in this gear and ensure that any naked parts are appropriately padded with something that closely resembled talcum powder with a piece of cloth two inches wide? I didn't fancy my chances in a real scenario. Suddenly, someone screamed, "Gas, gas, gas," at which point we'd hit the floor and have to put on our mask within nine seconds (thankfully not while going to the toilet). After which we would have to endure the delights of the gas chamber test. I hated it. Having to take off your mask in a cloud of CS gas, clean it and put it on again, all with your eyes closed and without breathing, was something we dreaded. I managed it every year bar one. That year I could not work out which way up the mask was or where the straps were, and ended up taking a lungful of the pungent, bitter gas. As I was let out I vomited, and couldn't work out what was the worst thing: my lungs screaming or my eyes burning. The following years, I dreaded it even more, but there was no choice. During my training, if I heard the words "character developing" one more time I think I might have screamed.

Bizarrely, despite us being in an environment where the perception was that we barked orders at people, telling them what to do, I never did. In sixteen years, I never once *told* anyone to do anything; I asked. However, because we had rules, maybe we knew that the request was not just a request. So maybe the order was implied. I don't know. It was very different and yet the same as my upbringing, because there I was clearly told exactly what to do and what not to do, but I also knew the rules and what might happen if they were broken. The military world was a comfortable place to be. Yet, far from fearing it, I had a sense of belonging; a camaraderie I have not experienced in any job in Civvy Street. For some of our colleagues and bosses, we would go to the ends of the earth and back for them.

I say 'for some'. There were the few who led by fear. They thought being a badass was a way to show power. Fortunately they were few and far between. I also learned that standing up for yourself didn't get you far in this hierarchical organisation. On one such tour – my first, in fact – I was working for a man who was vile. Even now, if I saw him I would cross the road rather than talk to him, not out of fear but out of a lack of respect. I only realised late into my tour that he had wanted a fighter controller (one of his own kind) in the newly created post, not an Admin Sec officer, which was what he got. Working in a bunker, where often I'd go to work and go home in the dark without seeing daylight during my shift, I was given a tiny square table in the corner of a room, no computer and no terms of reference for the job. I was straight out of training and had no idea what I was doing. Most mornings I had to receive my orders in a gruff, barky kind of way. Sometimes my boss would shout; sometimes I had to wear my hat to receive his onslaughts and sometimes not. He was never nice. Once, over drinks in the Sergeants' Mess, he said to me: "My view was that you would either sink or swim, and you swum." I asked what would have happened if I'd sunk. His reply: "Tough."

The lowest point was my annual reviews, which in those days could be written without being shown to the individual. This, of course, resulted in many people realising later that what they had been told was not the truth. I am sure many had a shock when, under the Freedom of Information Act, they could ask for copies of their reports. On one of mine it was said that I "was of average height and average weight, which served the false impression that I was overweight". What the fuck was it with men and their fixation on my body size? If it was false, why mention it at all? I remember asking my Wing Commander at the time how he thought this was useful, as by this stage I had complained about my boss and demanded to see my report. I think my exact words were: "What would you like me to do? Lose three stone in weight" —I was not overweight at all— "or pop myself in a baby bio bag to grow for a few weeks?" He had no real answer and spluttered something about agreeing it wasn't useful, but the sentence remained. The reason for my annoyance and speaking to my Wing Commander, in effect breaking the chain of command, was that I found out my own staff had been asked to type my report up, and apparently it was meant to be much worse but the words wouldn't fit in the box.

Oh, lucky me. I learned another important thing on that tour. Loyalty. It isn't given, it's earned. The same with respect – which was exactly how I felt about my parents. They didn't deserve my respect because they never gave it.

There is no doubt about it: that tour took a toll on my mental health, although that was something that was never discussed. You were considered weak if you suffered mental issues. After the death of my mum and the subsequent birth of my first child, I was sent to a psychiatric unit to talk about what had happened. It was clear I wasn't myself. I kept getting sick and felt down. This might have been some kind of depression, but I was so good at papering the cracks I didn't allow myself to think like that. The mere fact that the psychiatric building was on an operating base, though, led me to close up and pretend everything was fine, rather than be seen to walk in and out of there, be labelled and have my career damaged. I have no proof that would be the case but, listening to other people talk, it seemed likely. As well as rules, there were judgements and assumptions.

My first tour lasted nearly two years, and my confidence was worn away as I did my best to cope with a horrible situation. Others saw how I was being treated and tried their best to help, but couldn't do much. Those of non-commissioned rank who were my colleagues could not tell a commissioned officer what to do, no matter how much they wanted to. One very kind Petty Officer drove me to the local village in his car one day and we just sat and chatted overlooking the sea. He said: "No one should be treated like you are being." He engineered a trip for me to Cyprus and Gibraltar for three weeks on HMS *Invincible* as a way to escape, even for a short time. Another lesson learned: someone you least expect can have your back. There is always some kindness. I always prided myself in getting on with people, looking after them and listening. Some served me with the same treatment in return.

Still, everything passes with time. Finally, given a new job to go to, I stuck two fingers up at the place I had worked for two years and moved on to my next posting, where I went from strength to strength, regained my confidence and loved my work. I gained many skills from then on, including project management and people management. I was promoted and had a fabulous time along the way; but, just like that first tour, nothing lasts forever. Just like that, sixteen years disappeared in front of my eyes. It was time to move on, turn the page and start a new chapter.

What might this mean for you?

- If you have a setback or disappointment with a job opportunity, how does this affect you? How much do you take it to heart? How much does it make you fear trying again?

- What new skills could you gain that might help you get your dream job or change your profession?

- What behaviours in the workplace have you, or do you, put up with and why? How could you behave differently to change those behaviours?

- What help could you seek from others so that you don't have to face things alone?

Chapter 6

Suicide – let's not sugar coat it

The weather in November was enough to serve as a reminder, warping me back to that weekend. The memory was etched on my brain like an indelible mark, never to be forgotten. I put my hand over my bump. "Let's go home for some TLC," I whispered. For a second there was a flicker in my head, wondering if this was actually possible; but surely the thought of a baby arriving would ensure that better treatment was on hand. It was a long drive, but it seemed worth it.

At seven months pregnant, with my husband working overseas, I had decided to visit my parents before I couldn't fit behind the steering wheel anymore. Now I was married I was 'allowed' to have the double room at the back of the house, which felt weird because it wasn't my room and, to my knowledge, no one apart from my grandad had ever slept there. To be fair, though, sleeping in a single bed on my side (my favourite position) might well have seen my stomach fall over the side of the mattress. Like watching molten glass drop on the end of the rod, heavy and slow. So it was a blessing in disguise, even though I felt like I was staying at a guest house rather than what had been my childhood home.

It was a Friday, and after a five-hour drive I arrived home in the early afternoon with a sense of relief and with anticipation of the weekend ahead. I popped my things upstairs, giving a sideways glance to what was my old room. I wasn't sure what I thought about it. It looked so small now compared to when I lived here, and yet it hadn't changed a bit. It certainly didn't hold any nice memories. I stared at the chair mocking me in the corner, shook the feeling off and went back downstairs, but there was something off. It was barely noticeable, but the shifts in mood in this house were always noticeable. Perhaps I was just attuned to it. There were no words spoken between Mum and Dad, which was nothing new. But Mum seemed to be on edge – nervous somehow. She seemed to be fretting about everything (more so than normal). I could feel my eyes starting to roll.

Mum banged away in the kitchen sorting supper (must be fish; Friday was always a fish day), so I swapped a few perfunctory sentences with Dad. Far from feeling relaxed, I had the feeling I might have been better off staying at home and resting. It felt like a wave of nausea I had to clamp down and push away. I had no idea why I had imagined that staying here would be a good idea, but I always lived in hope.

Supper was brief and quiet, the three of us around the tiny square table in the kitchen. For us all to eat round it, one person had to get in first and then the table was moved into place. It was like a game. Not for the first time, I felt trapped. The irony of trying to fit around the table was not lost on me because behind was the dining room, used only once a year on Christmas Day. My aunt had been unwell in hospital with a brain tumour.

Mum said: "Well, what if your father suggests your aunt stays with us?"

I asked: "Has he said that is the case?"

Mum answered: "No, but—"

I asked: "Well then, it's not an issue until he mentions it, and to be honest, she is his sister and you have space, so what is the issue?"

Mum said: "You just don't understand – she smokes!"

For those who remember Hyacinth Bucket from the TV programme *Keeping Up Appearances*, that is exactly how Mum sounded when, to her, something was totally incredible.

That was the start of the evening. Mum spent most of it after supper frantically knitting jackets for the baby. I kept telling her there was no rush, it could wait until after the baby was born. She kept knitting. Then she got on to the subject of Dad.

"You don't understand what it's like to live with him," she shrieked.

Well, that was just plain stupid. Of course I did! It's why I left home. My answer was simple although, in hindsight, a little trite. "So do something about it, then!"

At that point I had had enough. This wasn't what I had come home for. Far from being relaxing, it was proving to be stressful. Raking stuff up I had long left behind was not proving useful. I went to bed, but en route added I had decided to go back to RAF Marham the next day, and I explained my reasons why – not in a mean way, but for once I felt I was looking out for myself. I was standing up for myself, child vs parent. However, if I had known that would be the last time I would see her, I might have acted differently. Perhaps a hug might have been more appropriate...

I packed the car the next morning and told Dad I was leaving. Mum was nowhere to be seen. I assumed she had gone shopping or stomped off to be by herself, so I left and returned to the RAF base late afternoon. It was November so it was dark by then, and I phoned Dad to see if Mum was back. Nothing. I asked him to check the hospitals just in case and suggested that on her return we get her to see the doctor, because I felt she might be depressed. I'd been thinking about her behaviour on the long drive back and thought there was something wrong. She seemed manic or furtive in her behaviour. To be honest, at thirty-five I knew nothing of depression and how it could manifest itself. It was just a feeling. From what I know now, it could have been related to the menopause and/or her diabetes. She was quite happy to talk about the latter, but 'menopause' barely existed as a word at that time. It could also have been as a result of being stuck in a life she didn't want and felt she had no control over. By the time I went to bed there was still no news, and I was worried. There was a storm and it was cold and windy. No one should be out in that, I thought.

It wasn't the first time she had gone out with the intention of worrying us. She used to go off on her bike, cycle out to her mother's grave out in the country, and then return. Well, at least, she would say that was where she had been. No one actually knew. She always came back, and normal service would be resumed. I think she wanted someone to go to find her, rescue her and tell her that everything was going to be OK, and then she would come back happy. Of course, it never turned out like that. Her face wore years of pain on it – in the furrowed brow, the lack of life behind the eyes, and the grim-faced smile.

On the Sunday, I had a call from Dad, who said she still hadn't appeared back home and wasn't in hospital. I went into denial. I knew instinctively what had happened, but I told him that if she didn't reappear by lunch I'd come back home, at which point his friend took the phone and gently said: "I think you should come home now." Well, that did it. I had to face reality and couldn't put it off. I spoke to my work colleague and explained I needed to make the return trip home as my mum had disappeared. I remember talking in a very calm, detached way. I remember taking a break on the journey back at a service station and thinking how strange it was that life for me had been turned upside down and everyone else was bustling about with their business as normal. It felt as though the exterior world was silent and I could only hear the thoughts in my head.

It wasn't long after I returned home that we had the call from the police saying that they were going to visit our house. She had been reported missing and was a diabetic who would need insulin. What followed was amusing to me in a macabre way. They searched the sheds, attic, garage, maybe for evidence that we had finished her off – because, as we are told, most murders are carried out by people known to the victim. At the same time they told me that, in my condition, I should try to eat something. So, while they questioned me about my parents' marriage and the events leading to her disappearance, there I was, bold as brass, eating beans on toast in the dining room. My mum would have been beside herself. The dining room that was only for Christmas, and here I was eating in it on a normal Sunday evening like I owned the place. Dreadful behaviour. I was kind of inwardly smirking.

"How would you describe your parents' relationship?" I was asked.

"Volatile," I replied. What else could I say? That they loved each other? Couldn't be without each other? I mean, I knew he hadn't killed her, but I wasn't going to pretend that this was love's young dream.

She was found, with her arms crossed across her chest, dead

in a copse about a quarter of a mile from our house a few hours later. Apparently, a man walking with his bird of prey found her. Poor guy. We assumed she had taken an overdose of insulin and gone to sleep. We have no proof, though. She was a diabetic, had threatened suicide before, and always said she had an easy way out. I can't even remember what the verdict was: death by misadventure, maybe. But it certainly didn't confirm suicide. I remember the policewoman trying to persuade my dad not to go to identify her. In my mind then I assumed she had been pecked by birds or other creatures. In the end his brother went, confirmed it was her and reported that she looked peaceful.

My husband was working overseas. I phoned him and said: "They have found my mum."

"That's great," he said.

"Not really – she is dead. They found her in a wood," I answered.

"Do you want me to be with you?" he asked.

Another one of those millisecond moments where I thought of a number of responses I would rather have heard. 'I'll be on the next flight out' or 'oh my God, how awful, are you OK?' To be fair, he would also have been in shock, and to him it was simply a question, to which I could have just responded 'yes please'. But in the time it took to think of that, I'd said: "No, it's fine. I'd rather be alone."

I was tired. This was bullshit. In that moment, I didn't care what anyone thought. I just wanted a normal response to an abnormal situation. In the end, he came and didn't know how to act all weekend, so it was pretty dreadful. I'm sure it was uncomfortable for him, as he probably felt like a spare part in a very unusual situation, but it probably didn't touch the sides of the way I felt. I just thought, *Why couldn't you just stay where you were, I can cope much better by myself*, pretty much like I had always felt I had done.

The rest is a haze. I remember staring outside the lounge window and the overwhelming feeling was one of relief. One part of the emotional roller coaster had stopped. Meanwhile my dad started talking about her, this "amazing woman", as though she was the biggest love of his life. He wouldn't stop. The vicar came round, and all my dad could do was regale stories about how wonderful she was. Maybe that was a way to assuage his guilt? Who knows? I never asked. At one point my dad looked at me and said: "She was so wonderful, wasn't she?" My brain went on a treasure hunt, searching for the wonderful memories, and came up blank. All I could remember was the lack of touch, no hugs, hurtful, spiteful words and someone who, frankly, was most definitely not my protector. I remember thinking that I had never seen my dad lift a finger to my mum – it was only me who became the punchbag for all the disappointments he felt with his life. My response was, "If you insist." The vicar was a wily old fox, and he shifted in his seat. I offered a cup of tea. He followed me into the kitchen and very quietly said: "If you ever need to talk, you know where I am."

He was so kind. I could have cried there and then, but I never did talk to him. Was that a mistake? I don't know. But I had never told anyone anything about my life behind these walls. How could I tell a complete stranger now? How would it help?

In some ways I felt stupid, I think; I felt that if the words came tumbling out of my mouth, they would seem inconsequential, if not trivial, to others and I would be told to 'pull myself together' or to stop moaning. I had kept the words inside me for so long, they literally would have had to be prised out. Even as a fully grown adult, I still felt scared that my words would brand me a liar and I would be shot down in flames, with disastrous consequences. Of course, this was all in my mind. Who knows what might have happened if that same vicar had stepped forward, hugged me (dammit, that would have definitely made me cry) and suggested a time and a place to meet? If he had taken the time to open up the clam that was me. I am not blaming him at all. I just know that often a question sometimes needs to be asked in different ways to elicit a response.

I don't even think I cried at the funeral. My dad, meanwhile, was sobbing, seemingly finding it difficult to stand. I was finding it difficult to understand that, and remember thinking *What are you doing? Why on earth are you crying?*

My refusal to cry felt defiant and easy at the same time. In one way I wonder if I felt he was partly responsible for her death; but to be utterly fair to him, she, I think, broke psychologically after she gave birth to me. I have no real proof of this, just talk from my dad when I was in my twenties that he felt she had done her duty. I suspect, because of her inability to show physical love to me, a sense of permanent detachment, and the fact that her mum died in the same year I was born, that she might have suffered post-natal depression, but it is just that – a suspicion. In another way, did she deserve my tears, leaving me again unsupported (as an adult, like she had done when I was a child) and pregnant at seven months, about to embark on the journey of motherhood? Again, unlikely, as she was hardly the shining example of a loving mother. Finally, I really think it was because I wanted to protect my baby. I consciously decided that despite this massive shock, her actions were not going to affect what was growing inside my belly.

I was shocked by the number of people spilling out of the

church. Were they here because they loved her or because her death was news? I could hear people whispering. "Why couldn't she wait for her grandchild?" "How do you think she did it?" "Do you think he was the reason why she did it?"

I remember the support of my cousin, who at various stages said: "You aren't going to like this bit." After losing her father, she understood what it was like to bury a parent. There were people coming up to me sobbing, including people who purported to be my godparents, whom I hadn't seen in over twenty years, wailing, snot running down their faces. I just found it all a bit surreal and sycophantic. The wake was like any other – laughs and chats. Inside I felt empty. In two months my first baby would be born. Those two knitted jumpers would never be worn – secreted into a box for safekeeping lest they be spoilt in the wash, or was it because I couldn't bear to be reminded that she had existed? There would be no grandmother on this side of the world to welcome him. Just a grandfather that I would never, ever leave my children in the company of, alone.

I headed back to the base where I worked. I remember thinking that I had to hold it together for my baby. It was to be my undoing several years later. What struck me was that no one knew what to say. People were mortified, embarrassed, sad for me, sad for my unborn child. It wasn't that people in the military didn't deal with death or weren't understanding, but it was the circumstances – suicide. I understood that, but inside I was screaming for people to talk to me, to act as though it was a more normal kind of death. Some just gave me a hug but no words. That was lovely. In that moment, no words were needed. People just thought it would be too painful to talk about, so didn't. I wish there wasn't so much stigma surrounding it. I didn't know what to say to my dad, and vice versa, so we just left it until many years later. I had no siblings, so my thoughts were my own.

I feel no anger and, bizarrely, no guilt. I say 'bizarrely' because we did argue the night before. I simply feel she was ill. Sometimes I have the feeling that I wish she had left a note by way of explanation, but usually I have a sense of acceptance as to the reasons she took her own life. I feel she had been planning it all along and that, even if I had prevented her from doing it on that occasion, she would have succeeded another time. I felt she yearned for a release from this life and she got it. She was worried about dying from something horrible associated with her diabetes and had already started to show early signs of kidney failure. Knowing what I know now, and having gone through depression myself, yes, a hug might have been more useful for her that night than basically telling her to man up. She, like me, was keeping her thoughts to herself, not wanting to burden others or ruminate on her thoughts, which she felt were her own to resolve. I might have been curious and asked what she was most worried about and tried to understand her resistance in seeking help for some ailments. However, I was in child mode and having lived with years of this behaviour, I am not even sure this would have changed the outcome. If someone isn't willing to open up and engage we can't make them, and I certainly didn't have the skills at that time to try. But I've never dwelled on it; my mum made a choice.

What I have been mindful of is that you never really know what is going in someone's mind, and that you can live with someone or be close to them and yet not know them at all. Talking to people, really talking to them and finding out how they are, is key to understanding. Many years later I was struck by a conversation I had with my second husband, as we realised that as children we didn't really care about our parents' lives or, as already mentioned, grandparents' either. We didn't question their past. Their past was boring. Our future was exciting. So many unsaid emotions, thoughts and influences. We don't like to see our parents sad or afraid. It makes *us* sad and afraid, and we don't want to think or be like that. As adults we tend to live in reality, whereas a child's life is often imagination and make-believe. It's not that, as children, we don't care; we just don't have the awareness or possess the communication skills. Parents or other adult figures are there from the start; whether that is a positive or negative experience, they are just 'there'. No questions seem necessary. So we don't delve, pick the scab to see what is under the surface, and adults – being adults – keep the information close. They guard it like a secret. Not intentionally but because they may not want to worry their children or because they simply can't find the words. Inevitably it can result in an invisible, impenetrable wall. Given the two worlds, is it any wonder that we can't see what is in front of our eyes? Persuading people to seek help means we must also recognise help is needed and we, when we are close to it, can't always give it. What it did make me wonder later was: would that be me? Can suicide run in families? If it was depression, does that mean I will get it? I had no answers, only questions, but they were questions voiced only in my head.

Being able to discuss it more openly, rather than feeling I was the one being talked about in hushed whispers ("Ah bless, did you hear what happened to her mum? I wonder why she did it"), really would have been more helpful. I didn't need it to be sugar-coated. I knew what she had done. What I needed was to voice how I felt about it.

What might this mean for you?

- If you have experienced the suicide of a family member, loved one or friend, how has it impacted your life?

- What help have you sought to cope with the impact and emotions?

- How has it made you consider mental health issues?

- If people around you are struggling and not talking, how might you become curious about their world to understand how they are feeling?

- If you find that you are keeping thoughts to yourself about suicide or harming yourself, what is it that might prevent you talking to others or seeking help?

Chapter 7

A Mother's Love

A lioness with her cubs. That's what I think of. I went to Tanzania for my fiftieth. On my birthday, on a drive, I witnessed a lioness losing one of her cubs to prowling hyenas. The cub was being brave and independent, and sadly paid the price. But the crying of the mother…that sound…

For ages she cried for her cub and refused to stop looking, rushing towards the hyenas to keep them away from her other cub. That's what a mother's love means to me. Not to be ignored, mistreated – or worse, left to experience mistreatment at someone else's hands, with no intervention. You would do anything to defend your own. I tried to find a quote that would sum up a mother's love, but none of them felt right when compared to my experience, and all of them seem to transcend mothers to another place, far away from what I can even begin to imagine. So I looked up examples of how parents generally show love for their children and tried to align them with my own experiences…

Putting food on the table and a roof overhead. Yes, that was provided. Even if the food was a little dodgy or samey, there were three meals every day. My mum's cooking was sometimes remembered for all the wrong reasons! I recall one day at supper when my mum was cooking an omelette. Every day she would also cook stewed fruit, with no sugar, and sometimes we would have custard (with sweetener) – I can tell you are getting the vibe of how tasty these dishes were. On this particular day, she couldn't understand why the omelette wouldn't solidify. Eventually, and as if this was totally acceptable, she began pouring the omelette over our vegetables. Suddenly she started laughing. It wasn't something we heard that often, but it was a real laugh; in fact, we started smiling for no reason, even though the yellow liquid on our plates was congealing and looked like a scientific experiment that had gone wrong.

"What is the matter?" asked Dad. Holding the pan, with tears streaming down her face, she cried: "I've cooked the custard." So now it all made sense. The 'omelette' was in fact our dessert. I have no idea what we ate that night instead – probably sandwiches – but that moment stuck in my head for ever. Probably because it was a happy one, yet a rare one. I don't remember any of us, including her, thinking she had failed in any way, but just that she was a human being who had made a simple mistake that was utterly hilarious.

I've also put food on the table and provided a roof over our heads, and since the boys were three and five I've done it alone. At one point, after my dad died, my bank account read zero. There was no inheritance, and Dad's house in Spain couldn't be sold, due to economic issues. The cost of being able to inherit it took up all of my savings and, even when I did manage to rent it for a few years, by the time I'd had to pay for decorating, repairs and other costs, there was very little left. I eventually sold the house for about £30,000 just to get rid of the stress it created. I'm guessing I broke even.

I had no family and no one to ask for help in terms of money. I just had my job, thank goodness, but the fear of losing it all and the stress it created was exhausting. I never told the boys. They didn't need to know. It was my responsibility to ensure I looked after them. So, in an effort to make sure food was on the table and a roof was over our heads, I worked hard. I don't just mean at work. I did work at home when the boys had gone to bed – not every night, but more than I care to admit. I did all the cooking, refused to have loads of takeaways, and cooked everything from scratch. For quite a few years the boys thought McDonald's was an ice cream shop, not a fast food store.

I have no idea if my mum put my needs – those of her only child – first, before her own, or in fact made any sacrifices. Maybe? I think she focused on being a housewife and a mum, but more of a housewife. I often thought that her way of caring must have been through looking after the house and putting food on the table. Perhaps that is what she was taught – I don't know. In terms of work, she wasn't – or didn't appear to be – ambitious, although I am aware she felt hampered by her diabetes. She did have jobs: she was a secretary for years, and I remember, in the holidays, sitting next to her, playing with toys or creating some hideous woolly snake from a bobbin with four little nails hammered into its top. These were the days before 'childcare' was a thing, but I was always quiet, and I remember the pickled cucumber sandwiches for lunch and the walk home. Rarely was I annoyed or sick. The floor where she worked was wooden and the room was bare. The only things in that room were a desk, which my mum sat at, and two chairs. One for her and one for me. On the desk was a typewriter, and I used to be fascinated by the clicking of the levers and watching the words appear on the paper. It felt quite magical.

Mr Rogers (I've no idea who he was or what he did) used to poke his head round the door occasionally and make some enquiries. He always reminded me of one of the Wombles because his glasses were always perched on the end of his nose. He seemed nice, though. My mum was always polite.

Maybe the trick was that she never made me aware of her sacrifices. Never spoke about them. As parents, we want to protect our children from hardship and pain, so we keep it to ourselves. I knew my mum had once wanted to decorate cakes and was somehow prevented from doing so because of her diabetes. But whether she was frustrated in not having a career, I have no idea. In truth, I never thought to ask. She was just 'Mum', and she was also from an era when it was common for women to stay at home and look after their kids and not even question it – not overtly, anyway.

I've always wanted a career so that financially I have not had to sacrifice my own needs. I do remember buying my own clothes at charity shops to save money, but I refused to do so for the boys. I did sacrifice my own emotional and health needs, and if I had my time over again I would have done things differently. As well as working, I'd sort all the stuff required for school and do all the ironing and washing and cleaning.

Feeling that I had to do everything and keep going even if I felt under par as a mum stemmed from when I was young. On the rare occasions I was sick, my mum would come into my room and remove my bookcase. She would search under the mattress for any books I might have secreted. She would purse her lips and say: "If you are sick, you are sick and shouldn't be reading or doing anything else." So I would drag myself to school, doing anything other than stay at home to endure days in bed with nothing to do but sleep, stare or think. That was not helpful for me in the future. I didn't usually realise when my body needed rest, and even when I did, I would fight it. During my breakdown, which I had not recognised I was heading towards, I am not sure I was a great person to be with, although my boys don't seem to remember anything in particular about that time. Sacrificing my own health and mental well-being by driving myself so hard doesn't seem such a sensible thing to do when I look back. It's certainly taught me a lesson – one I wish I need not have learned.

What I learned through NLP training was that my own drivers had contributed in a big way to how I operated. I did all the things my mum did, on top of working full-time and worrying about my appearance. My inbuilt drivers of working hard, standing on my own two feet, working when sick, being strong and being slim, coupled with fear of the consequences of not doing and being those things, kept me driving myself to a tempo that my body and mind could not keep up with. Through NLP I learned boundaries. Through hypnotherapy I learned to recognise priorities. Through counselling I learned how to be kind to myself and be proud of coming through the other side of not only depression but my childhood.

Flexibility is key to being a parent, with a willingness to change and adapt. There was no flexibility in our household. Not with set mealtimes, choice of meals, days for cleaning certain rooms and even how many times you could open the fridge (yes, really – and this got worse over the years). There were rules in the house. I wasn't allowed to put up posters in my room as it would mark the walls. There was an overriding rule: 'while you live in our house, you live by our rules and regulations'. I wasn't out every night, and when I did go out I was not home really late; but if I missed my curfew, I was locked out. That was it. Game over. To teach me a lesson, apparently. All it created was resentment, and it built up in me to the extent that I was so sick of hearing it I did leave to live somewhere else.

Even my mum's body had no flexibility. It was rigid; if I hugged her she would remain lifeless, arms down by her sides, expressionless the majority of the time. If she was cleaning, I was interrupting. I stopped hugging. I mean, I don't get that. If someone hugs me, I can't not hug them back. But who knows what was going on in her mind? Like me she was an only child, but probably in a much more austere, protected environment – although again I'm guessing and I don't know why I assume that, because my grandad, her dad, was really, really lovely. I never knew my grandmother, as she died just after I was born, and maybe that had something to do with my mum's demeanour or, as we would know it, post-natal depression.

I remember writing a message to my eldest son once in which I said: "I may not be perfect, but as you may discover one day, we do the best we can with the tools we have in the box." That is what I used to say about my parents. That they knew no better. That they did the best they could. I'm not sure I totally buy into that, because I believe everyone has a choice. I chose to parent differently, for example, but it was the story I told myself, otherwise things would have felt a lot worse, I am sure. However, I do think with my own boys I have been flexible. I don't have rules. Well, actually, I thought I had rules until, when I said that out loud one day, both of my boys nearly wet themselves laughing. "You so don't have rules!" they cried. OK, maybe I don't, but what they don't like doing is disappointing me, so I still like to think my 'big' rules are implied. As a result, though, there is no tension, no slamming of doors, no big shouty arguments. I'm not saying we don't argue – of course we do – but it doesn't go on for days. There is no violence.

I also admit when I am wrong, and I try to put myself in their shoes and remember what it was like to be young. NLP taught me that. I've had one instance of my eldest slamming doors. It started suddenly and there was no apparent reason for it. Stomping, accompanied door slamming and a face that would make Darth Vader wither. After a few days, as I was sitting on the sofa and the door slammed for the umpteenth time, I was just about to shout "Stop slamming the fucking door!" when something made me stop. I got up and went to follow him, but en route I went past the mirror. But it wasn't my face I saw; it was as though I was seeing my son's face, covered in spots. In my NLP training this would have been known as the mother of all examples of 'perceptual positioning', meaning to put yourself in the other person's shoes but in a way where you imagine you see out of their eyes and feel what they feel. In that split moment, I looked at the face in the mirror and instinctively knew what the problem was. My mouth made an 'O' shape and suddenly I realised. Going into my son's room, I sat on the bed and said: "I'm so sorry." He turned to look at me. "I remember going to school and if one spot dared to appear on my face I would feel devastated, ugly and feel that everyone was looking," I said. Tears welled up in his eyes. "Is that how you feel, love? Because honestly, I don't think you have 'just spots', I think it might be acne. Would you like to go to the doctor to see if he can help?" He nodded his head, and we had a hug.

From that day on, there was no door slamming, just a silence that came with being understood. I could have made it a whole lot worse by shouting because his actions annoyed me, but what I actually did was try to save him from pain.

I imagined that other people's parents were always on call and, throughout their lives, always in their corner. But I think my parents were glad when I left home. We never spoke about it, and I don't have one single memory of asking for help. Even when I went to music college, we had this thing called covenants. It was where you had financial assistance so if your parents gave you money, the government would also give a percentage of the required amount to help. One summer, aged eighteen or nineteen, I had nowhere to live. I had to move out of halls and the place I normally lived in was not available, so I asked my parents if I could come home for the summer. They seemed happy enough, but I don't know what went wrong. I remember arguments starting not long after I arrived. I was working all summer, so I wasn't at home much. One day there was a huge argument – I have no idea now what about – but yet again I was the punchbag. I phoned up work and said I would be late in (I was in no fit state) and I cycled to the family whom I had previously lodged with, who as soon as I entered thrust a glass of whisky in my hand. I was grateful for the warmth going down my throat and the feeling of relaxation it gave my tense body. I remember them saying to me: "We don't understand how you have been brought up in this environment and come out normal." Was I normal? I had no idea. But I felt broken.

I made it to work – at that point it was at a hotel – and asked if they had any staff accommodation. They didn't, so reluctantly I stayed at my parents' home and made sure I kept out of the way. Now, maybe I did start the argument – I have no idea. I was not a selfish or demanding child. Normally I didn't start anything – it would be in defence of some stupid rule or a horrible comment. That night when I went back, I saw my mum with a bottle of gin and tablets, sitting in the lounge, staring out of the window. I scurried away. I went into denial. Like all the other times she had threatened to commit suicide, she never had, and I couldn't see why this would be any different. The next day there she was, as large as life, as though nothing had happened.

I went back to college early, and as punishment for my 'behaviour' that summer my dad refused to pay my covenant for the term. I was not the kind of student who went out every night partying, so I didn't spend a lot. That money helped me buy food and survive. I was angry – livid, in fact. Angry because, even if I had retaliated, I know I didn't start the argument. I knew they still argued when I wasn't even there. But there I was, hands clenched, just like I did all those years ago, under the table, keeping it all in. Very calmly I said, "So when we get to Christmas, if we have an argument, will you take the Christmas presents back?" Dad turned and left. I was lucky not to receive another smack across the face, but we were outdoors, so he probably thought better of it.

My children are my children. Nothing will take that away from me. Nothing… I've been there during sick times, bad times and good times, and I like to think that I have a good relationship with them. I don't believe in being 'friends' with your children necessarily, but I have been there to give support, offer advice, give guidance and, most importantly, listen. I've brought them up to be independent, to live their own lives, but in essence I will always be their mum until I draw my last breath.

NLP has taught me to listen and to view life through their lens, not just through mine. How many times do we say we are listening, only to really be thinking of the next point we want to make? How many times do we stop and wonder what impact our words or even our tone might be having? Imagine if my mum had had access to such therapies, tools, training or social media which vocalised parenting skills. Might our relationship have been any different? Quite possibly; but I still can't shake off the feeling that one knows right from wrong. I didn't have any therapy until I broke, yet I was still able to show affection to my children, to kiss them, to hold them, to love them. I remember one hug in my childhood. One. It's not meant to be a 'go me, aren't I so perfect!' It's merely recognition that fundamentally we know what children need, because we were all children once. It might have helped us understand each other and communicate better, though, especially through those teenage years that are difficult for parents and their children to navigate.

I don't view parenthood as something where I hold the power over my children. From an early age I knew they had a voice and an opinion and feelings. I knew, because I remembered being young and having those same feelings and having my opinions quashed because they didn't appear to matter. For a while I had forgotten, but my NLP training flicked that switch once more and I had the power to imagine myself the same age as them, seeing life as they saw it, and we would work things out together. Now I'll go walking with them, and whatever worries they might have they spill the beans, and later they will say: "I don't feel as half as bad now." That gives me a warm, fuzzy feeling inside. A listening ear and soft tones are priceless.

The idea that parents provide protection from outside dangers was obviously not even in my parents' thinking. No. I was not safe from harm. I went to school with long-sleeved blouses to cover the broken veins of the last beating on my arm. I could not cover up the black eye, but no one asked anything.

If they had, I would just say "I fell over." I could not imagine telling the truth. I'd get into trouble for telling lies. I never used the word 'abuse'. It wasn't until I overheard my aunt saying it that I felt what the word meant. But I was scared I had over-egged it, and abuse was something really bad that happened to other kids and it didn't apply to me. What if it got out that I was using that word (in fact I was not the one who had said it in the first place)? What trouble would I be in? Would they take me away from my parents? On the one hand that thought was appealing, but on the other hand they were all I knew.

But I was not protected. I used to wonder about that later because I never saw my dad lay a finger on my mum. Not once. I don't think it's because I've buried it. I think I became the reason for his frustration. He had such hopes and dreams for me and for the way I was supposed to be that I guess he just felt bitterly disappointed. My mum did nothing to protect me. Nothing. She saved up her worst words when she was scolding – the worst, on occasion, being "slut" and "whore", and on what basis I have no idea – perhaps in response to how my actions at the time might have been seen in her upbringing. I had no boyfriend. I didn't kiss anyone until I was sixteen, so I had no clue. She had no emotional contact with me whatsoever, and she didn't protect me from my dad. I guess the last one was hard to do, but that didn't help me at all. There were no outside dangers that I could see. All the dangers were within the walls of my own home. When you don't feel safe in that place, it is hard to feel safe anywhere.

I remember sitting in the garden of our house on the RAF married patch with my baby in my arms. It was sunny and the air was nice and warm, with a fresh breeze across my face.

I was the typical proud first-time mother. I'd spent many years fearing being a parent. Now I couldn't imagine not being one. My health visitor had arrived for a check-up and she had brought a trainee with her. As we had tea, she went through a list of routine questions and also asked how I was coping, as my mum had committed suicide two months before Matt was born. I can't say it really affected me but, looking back, I might have been numb; I don't know, to be honest. I don't ever remember being upset. The only thing that had affected me was an episode of *Sex in the City* when the character Miranda was pregnant and her mum died just before she gave birth. I left the room, as it was too close to home. We had nearly finished going through everything when I suddenly looked at her and said: "How do I know I won't beat my child?"

The health visitor looked taken aback, and said: "Why would you think you would?"

"Because that is all I've known," I replied. The silence was palpable and the expression changed on her face. Tears started falling down my face, and she took my hand as I explained some things that had happened. If my entire childhood was stemmed in violence, how could I not do the same to my children? What would stop me?

"My dear," she said, "you won't do the same thing."

"How can you know that?" I wailed.

"Because we are sitting here having this conversation and you have recognised it," she said.

I wasn't sure I believed her, and I also wasn't comfortable about ever leaving my children with their grandfather, but her words comforted me in some way. I can't say it was easy. I had to make a choice, every day, *not* to beat my child, until it was no longer a choice but just part of me. Am I proud of that? Hell, yeah! I could have just repeated the patterns ingrained in me; but if my upbringing taught me one thing, I knew right from wrong. That is ironic, right? I didn't want any child to go through what I went through, so I chose to do something different.

With NLP I have learned we all have choice. We can choose to free ourselves from our past. We can choose to act differently, to make different choices. It is within our gift. It's the one thing I did without the aid of any therapy. I used my judgement and my innate sense of what was right and what was loving. I also learned that we adopt patterns of behaviour, and I have since heard this explained in an amazing way. We think, choose and feel. If you think of the brain as a responder, not a generator, it reacts to our thoughts. Doctor Caroline Leaf tells us that there are around 400 billion actions per second that make up that one 'think, choose and feel' moment. 400 billion per second! She asks us to think of our brain like a magnet and our thoughts as iron filings. Remember those as a kid? The patterns the filings created when they were attracted to the magnet? Once formed, they are there, intrinsically part of our being. They help create the narrative we tell ourselves, so depending on whether that narrative is negative or positive, that affects how we act. But we can break those patterns by working with our subconscious, and we can consciously decide to do so as well.

From that day in the garden, I used my conscious thought to break a pattern. Anyone who has come across James Clear's work *Atomic Habits* will understand the view that if you repeat something every day, it becomes much easier to develop new habits. I'd done it without realising. Since coming across NLP, I much prefer to work with the subconscious mind as the results can be far quicker, but I'm just glad I made the choice to do anything at all.

Did my parents teach me life skills? Yes and no. The discipline in my home stood me in good stead in terms of my work ethic and military life. I was excellent at timekeeping; I did as I was told; I didn't argue back; I spoke when I was spoken to; I had excellent manners; I ate everything put in front of me so as not to cause offence; I worked hard at school and always tried my best; I worked hard outside school and spent days in the holidays picking fruit in the fields among the wasps and the bees, filling up buckets of fruit, trying to get as much money as I could. I started a part-time job in a hotel at the age of fourteen and had to give half the money to my parents for my board. I knew right from wrong and lived in fear of being arrested for having done nothing at all! When I did do something wrong, I was beaten and shouted at. I was taught to be fearful. I'm not sure those are great lessons to teach your child. I was taught that men lay down the law and you do as you are told. That is definitely not a great lesson to teach your child in preparing them for personal relationships. I was never taught how to deal with money but was always made to feel that I had to pay them for the inconvenience I was causing. I couldn't have a hairdryer because it used too much electricity. My dad washed my hair until I was around fourteen because I'd waste too much water…and on, and on, and on.

I did get an apology from my mum once, and that inadvertently taught me how important it is to say that sometimes to our children. I can't remember what she said but it was some vicious comment, around the time I was taking my O levels. I scuttled upstairs to my room and could feel the tears smarting from my eyes. To my surprise, she came in and sat next to me. "I'm sorry," she said, "that was my fault, I shouldn't have said that," and gave me a hug. The one and only time. I've never forgotten it, and even when I think about it now it feels like yesterday. I just nodded, as I couldn't actually believe she had said it. I felt enormously sad afterwards that that was the only hug I can really remember. To not feel those hugs at any other time meant I clung onto that one memory.

I have some sayings in my home: 'Nothing is ever insurmountable'; 'don't forsake your health for money'; 'make money to make memories'.

My boys have had disappointments, setbacks and health issues, and I've tried to make them see that while these are indeed disappointments (I let them wallow a little), they rarely last for ever. We can use those experiences to learn. I do think it's important to acknowledge the failure and how that feels, but ultimately to turn it into a positive is much more useful. So if one of them didn't do well in a particular subject, we would examine alternative options. I remember once flying down the motorway (with a fair amount of road rage on the way) to get to Weston College, in Weston-super-Mare, in time for Matt to register his interest because they did the type of courses he wanted, only to realise it would be impossible for him to travel there. But we tried.

After my experiences with money and my own drivers, I've made sure that my boys understand not only the need to make money but also how to enjoy themselves. Earning money, to me, means it can help me create some memories for the memory bank. I'm not saying you can't do it without money, but if you are just making money for money's sake, what is the point? If you are making it just to survive, where is the fun in that? So either take your foot off the gas, even if that means you earn less (particularly if the effort is making you sick), or do something with it that makes you happy – and that doesn't mean spend all of it or gamble it away.

No one ever asked me about my day. They were not interested in my interests or dreams. Not ever, not as a child and not as an adult. No one ever asked me what I wanted to do. They had decided I was going to be the next James Galway. It's true they supported me in that – paying for lessons, buying a flute and piano so I could go to music college. But dreams? Don't be daft. Because I was never asked, I never thought to say what my dreams were. If I had, I'd probably have said 'an actress' and then believe that that was impossible, because actresses were pretty. So I went to music college. I can't say I enjoyed it. I was disciplined. I practised five to six hours a day and did my work, but writing essays about some crinkly old dead composer from 200 years ago didn't leave me enthralled by the subject. In truth, what I learned was that it was not about the writing of essays (hello, I'm writing a book, people) but about the subject matter. I fully suspect that if I had undertaken a psychology degree I would have had no such issue, but a crinkly old composer? No. Fast-forward five years, when I'd given up music one year after completing my degree, and I was off to London to start a new career in catering. To say my parents were disappointed was an understatement and they had no idea what to tell their friends. But, I figured, it was my life. They could either support me in that or not.

With my own children, I listened to them – not all of the time, but I always tried to take notice of what they were thinking, feeling or desiring. I flexed with their desires like grass bending in the wind. I've used my own skills and network to support them, even when things didn't quite pan out the way they expected. I've let them know that it's OK to write to me if talking face to face is difficult. Above all, I have held the theory that whatever they do, they will be just fine. I listen to them without judgement and offer guidance when needed. Obviously,

I'm not feckin' Mother Teresa. I am their mother. Correct. That means I can get things wrong sometimes, but I can also get things right. That makes me human. My curiosity increased with other people as well, I think, as I gained exposure to NLP and other learnings and I realised there is much more that lies behind the faces we see.

'Your child is your what? Your everything?' Wait. Rewind. Did I miss something? Was I in the wrong queue at birth, then? Hearing about your child's day…oh my God. In my world, growing up, I was the biggest irritation. No one was interested in my opinion. My opinion counted for zilch. I, probably like many children of that time, was told to go outside and play, preferably all day. On return we'd have a meal, my parents would talk, but children, seen and not heard, had no voice at the table. I have since learned about transgenerational trauma, which is when the experiences of parents affect the development of their children – and sometimes even their grandchildren. Also known as intergenerational trauma, it can show up biologically, socially, mentally or emotionally. It seems that it changes not only the way parents raise and relate to their children but also how certain genes are expressed in future generations. Anyway, who cared what I had done with my day, as long as my mum could continue with her cleaning tasks, and my dad was out working anyway? It makes me laugh now because even when I did ask my boys how their day was, they would say "Fine", as if nothing at all had happened at school. Playing with friends hadn't happened. Nothing, but at least I asked. Now, though, I can't shut them up!

I'm not sure I did anything that my parents found rewarding, other than music and the RAF. Parents' evening as a kid was a nail-biter. I'd hope and pray for good feedback so that I didn't suffer the consequences of not measuring up. Fortunately, in this area I was always spared. I worked hard at school. OK, I wasn't the brightest and, as I know now, I didn't learn well with the auditory style of teaching. I'd hear words for a while, but I couldn't sustain the concentration. I'd daydream, look out of the window and get lost in my own thoughts. But if the class was more visual or practical, that kept me connected and I found it much easier to learn. I'm not sure education has come on much over the years in accepting that we all learn in different ways. Certainly I didn't see much evidence of it at my son's school, but then, Christ, Shakespeare was still on the curriculum, for God's sake! I mean, how does saying 'where art thou?' link to a modern world of Instagram posts? Perhaps, through different learning methods, Shakespeare and the reason it might be important could be brought to life. I remember my English teacher (Mrs Bishop) introducing us to *To Kill a Mockingbird* when we were around fourteen. The way she brought it to life was to give us different parts to speak, and we all had to try an American accent. It was sometimes brilliant, often hilarious, sometimes serious and thought-provoking. She captured our attention, to the extent that even the most disruptive classmates were attentive and quiet.

I take time to listen to my kids' days, if they are forthcoming, even now they are grown up. There is gold dust in their words. Clues that enable you to know if there are underlying issues or not. I don't care whether it's about the part-time job, their studies or something else. I take notice because I love them and they deserve that. I note where I might have gone wrong with colleagues or friends in the past, and have shared those stories so they might not make the same mistake. I expect them to make some; I mean, it's impossible not to. But from those mistakes we learn. We adapt. We can forge a new future.

Parents are usually a child's biggest cheerleader, and when it came to concerts, plays and school events, my mum was always there. She might not have been whooping from the sidelines but she was always present. My dad came to some things grudgingly, usually to criticise afterwards. I used to just ignore him as this was really nothing new. Perhaps the reaction I needed and wanted wasn't there, so I learned to not bother but to 'be silent'.

I've no idea what they told friends, as I lost touch with most of them, including some of my family. When I left my home town, I deleted everything about it from the memory bank – which, sadly, meant deleting some people too. I've since reconnected with some of them, but it's a shame I wasted so many years without them in my life.

Sometimes what my parents told me would be different to what they told their friends. I remember applying to Dartington College of Arts and they came with me to visit it. People were wandering around with pink and blue hair, and instinctively I felt that this wasn't somewhere I would fit in. I've got no issue with hair colour; people can do with it what they want. But I hadn't fitted in anywhere in my life and I wanted to be somewhere that felt right. So I turned down my successful application, and my mum hit the roof. "If you think you are staying here while you sort yourself out, you have got another think coming." Well, I had no intention of staying there anyway, but that message was perfectly clear. Yet years later, when I was talking to a family friend, they said: "Oh yes, your mum told us about Dartington and how awful it was and she was so glad when you decided not to go." My face must have been a picture. Perhaps she felt that giving me a stern message would make me sort my life out and gain the independence she hadn't had. She might have felt sad that I didn't appear to be pursuing my dream, and maybe she was aware of how things were at home and was pushing for me to leave. Who knows?

There was one area they did agree on, and that was disappointment that I had given up music. I get it; they had supported me and paid for me in the years leading up to going to music college. But this was *my* life and choice and, while I enjoyed it, I could also take it or leave it.

There was no issue with me applying to the RAF. My parents were quite happy to crow to anyone about that; but a waitress in a restaurant – that was something they most definitely did not want to talk about. I understand they wanted more for me (so did I), but I needed a plan. As I was one of those kids who seemed to be a jack of all trades and master of none, at least that is what I was told, I needed to find my own way.

I'm proud of my kids' achievements, but not in the way you might expect. Their triumphs over personal issues. Their ability to have a strong work ethic despite sometimes serious health issues. I tell my kids I'm proud of them just for making it through what life throws at them. If I am not telling them, I write it down – spoken words can be forgotten, but written? That is much harder to do.

When it comes to education and work, the advice of my parents wasn't bad. I remember choosing my O levels and my parents advised me to explore a broad range of subjects, to keep my options open. It was good advice. Regarding work, my mum would say, "Don't leave a job until you have another one to go to." As a result, I have never been out of work. It's also something I've said to my children. But in general, I don't remember feeling supported. I remember getting my O level results. I got nine.

I didn't fail any, and they were all B and C grades. I was never an A-grade kind of gal. My mum's comment was: "Well, you obviously didn't work hard enough." My mouth wouldn't work, and all I could think of was how many hours, for days on end, I had sat upstairs in my room revising. However, what I know now is that my way of revising didn't help too much. I had a photographic memory. I could 'see' reams of information as it appeared on the page, including coffee-cup stains. What I couldn't do was thread different bits together. But did that mean I wasn't working hard enough? Hell, no. I worked. My mum got one O level at school, and later on when I reflected on that, I suspect her comment was because she wanted better for me. I'm just not sure that that kind of comment really helped. As a sixteen-year-old I had no clue about NLP or how to effectively communicate, and I never thought to ask her before she died. However, I felt hurt and misunderstood because I knew how hard I had worked. Of course I accept she wanted the best for me, but once again I had failed to make them proud. Knowing she had one O level felt incongruent with what I had achieved and the efforts I made.

My parents were not the type of people I went to for advice, especially Mum. Maybe it was because I didn't feel loved (in the way I needed) fundamentally, or maybe I just felt she didn't have any advice to offer. Also, as a child I had no concept of what love was, and there was a natural assumption that all parents love their children. The only person I relied on for support was me. I was taught to stand on my own two feet, and consequently learned to be independent. It was hard because I wasn't the most naturally confident person either, so being independent and unconfident meant I had to put more effort into it. That attitude was to have its drawbacks later when I didn't seek support or even know how to ask for it.

I want what is best for my children, and of course that means not worrying about money and how to survive. But most of all I want them to have a rich and fulfilled life, one that isn't necessarily burning them out on the continuum-to-success treadmill. No, I want them to savour their experiences, create lovely memories and to bask in the world they are in. That is their life.

A mother's love? My boys have had that in spades. That was my choice to give them that gift. To make sure that they knew they were loved, unconditionally, completely, and will be until I draw my last breath.

What might this mean for you?

- What are your emotions/feelings regarding your own mother?
- How might this have affected your own reactions towards other people personally and professionally?
- If you are able to appreciate that the way you react is only in response to the way you were taught, what would you unlearn given the opportunity?
- If you are a parent, have your own experiences changed the way you operate with your children?
- If you are a parent and could climb into the body of your child and see the world as they see it, how might that change your approach?

Chapter 8

Nine to Five

I'm not going to lie. From a young age I was ambitious, strong, and determined to succeed. I was brought up to believe you get nothing in this life for free and you have to work hard for what you get. I also learned that you saved up money if you really wanted something, and shouldn't pay for things you couldn't afford. That drove me to want money. Lots of it. I couldn't tell you how much was enough – just that I wanted more. Definitely more than my parents appeared to have had had. More, so that lack of money wasn't a constant reminder of what I didn't have. Maybe more, so that I could relax. The trouble was I never actually defined how much was enough, so I never knew when I'd reached my goal. It wasn't until recently that I felt I could relax and ask myself: "If you had to stop work tomorrow, would you be OK?" When the answer was yes, I could really feel my inner core relaxing. I can't remember a time when I felt like that before.

Maybe when I was married for the first time. I felt relaxed as we both had good jobs, but that was replaced by other stresses, so I can't say it was the most relaxing experience overall. Even then what was interesting is that we had each assumed that the way we were living was acceptable to the other person, when in reality the opposite was the case. My upbringing was lacking in precious memories. I saw money as a way to create lovely new memories. I'm not talking about extravagances here, just choices like going out for meals, staying in nice hotels, having nice holidays without trying to do it on the cheap. However, somewhere between my husband's need to save money and my need to have good memories, translations became lost, feelings were hurt, and negative memories were usually the result. When we divorced and met one time to chat about why we had ended this way, I remember responding to his statement of "But I was saving for our future, a nice house and no money worries" with "Well, I didn't know that – and to be honest, what about the here and now?" Not to be macabre, but we see premature death all the time, and my own experiences had taught me to take nothing for granted. What if there wasn't a future? What if we only had the here and now? I didn't mean spend everything we had, but acknowledge the present to create memories for our future.

After my divorce, I drove myself hard. I worked harder than ever, and that period of time was a massive change for all of us. Suddenly we were moving home, schools, county and, for me, job. I was doing it alone. I left the RAF because I couldn't see myself yanking two boys around different schools every two years or packing them off to their dad's for six months or more when I was on detachment. I wanted stability for them. Boarding school wasn't an option for me. I wanted to see their little faces every day. Leaving Matt's primary school in floods of tears was a sobering new start. Nevertheless, off we went to start our new adventure. It was Christmas, so on the way down to our new house we picked up a Christmas tree, which started the household tradition of buying a tree much taller than our ceiling, and the top had to be chopped off to fit. We never had a real tree at my parents' house, and only one during our married life, so I had no clue, when it came to size, what might be appropriate. I soon found out that ours was not. There was no room for an angel on our tree unless she straddled the top, facing towards the ground, tree shoved up her arse, with her back shoved against the ceiling and a look of outrage on her face. I think 2020 was the biggest tree ever, down to me waiting too long and lack of choice – post-Covid nightmare. I had to cut off about two feet!

That particular Christmas, though, on our first night in our new home, when I tried to pump up the air beds I couldn't understand why nothing was happening – until I realised that the stopper on the opposite side was out. That was the start of me realising what it was going to be like as a single parent – worn out and struggling to be everything to everyone. The boys were only three and five. I was trying my best to be upbeat and make it fun, when in reality I wanted to cry and spend twenty-four hours in bed. It was not the last time I would feel that way, but it did set a trend going forward.

I believe I made the right choice in getting divorced. For me, at least. But coming out of the back end of that (and I was grateful to my husband for making it as painless as possible) – the emotions associated with it, gaining new qualifications in project management to start my new job and leaving a life that I had known for sixteen years – was something I had hugely underestimated. But with my positive personality and dogged determinism at the ready, I started this new chapter with gusto. Well, as much gusto as I could summon.

I made a mistake not long after I started working part-time.

I asked for three days a week for six months and my company were obliging. However, I had never worked part-time in my life, and found myself checking emails and keeping on top of work on my days off. I know now the only person asking me to do this was me. Terrified of being out of a job, of being a failure, of not being perceived as a hard worker in a completely different environment where people didn't know me were all factors that drove me to continue working when I should have been relaxing and recovering. The most obvious point was that I was only being paid for three days a week; had I put those boundaries in place, maybe I would have prevented my ultimate breakdown by taking the time for me that I needed. At some point in the end I decided to work full-time. If I was, in effect, working full-time hours, I might as well be paid for them. An element of self-worth comes into play here, in that I considered that I would only be respected and admired if I worked really hard. I wanted to please everyone, bosses in particular. I wanted to be successful, I feared failure and often I didn't speak up for myself, which was, I think, directly related to my childhood, because speaking out had consequences.

Don't get me wrong, I did have some support over some of those early years. I had au pairs to take the boys to and from school, clean and occasionally babysit. Some of those au pairs I am still in contact with, as they left an impression on our lives, and we on theirs. It also opened the boys' worlds up to different cultures and habits. However, I was still the same doggedly determined person as always. I was afraid to give them too much to do in case they felt hard done by, complained about me (to friends and family) and left, so I tried to make life as easy as possible. I made it a rule that as soon as I was home, they were off duty and I was on mum duty. In essence, I started work all over again. Giulia, from Italy, made the most amazing salads in the summer, and that was a godsend. Every day a new type of salad would be prepared and I just had to arrive! It was bliss. Rachel, from New Zealand, treated the boys as if they were her own; Natalia, from Spain, extended her stay from six to eighteen months, taught Josh Spanish and invited us to her wedding some years later. Silja, from Iceland, made us dinner once, a popular meal in her country, which to our surprise was something akin to rice pudding in ours. We were later to visit her family in Iceland, where we had one of our best New Year's Eves, with the whole of Aryaki lit up in fireworks at midnight, but where they served up a sheep's head – oh, I wish I had taken a picture of Matt's face. There were some lovely times.

There were also some tricky periods, where either the individuals were running away from something and hadn't understood the demands of looking after someone else's children and keeping them entertained, or where they just believed they could take what wasn't theirs and use the house as a base to get another job. This meant they were barely covering the basics of my needs. I learned as time went by, and sacked a few along the way because it was tiring. If it wasn't working out for any of us, we had to call it quits. It's also hard sharing your house with someone who is not a friend or a family member, but I also understood it was hard for them too, especially when English wasn't their first language. I think I was caring, but again I probably put their needs ahead of mine. There is a recurring theme here, isn't there? I didn't want to come across as dictatorial; raising my voice meant that I would feel I was becoming my dad, so instead I was always the peacemaker and compromiser.

I hadn't been at my new job for long and had left my CV on the photocopier. As I went to retrieve it, I saw two men walking towards me looking at a piece of paper, smirking and talking. I instinctively knew it was my CV they had, and as I approached I said: "Is that mine?" When it was obvious that it was, I then asked: "Is there a problem with it?" Of course, they shook their heads emphatically and replied, "No." But their actions affected me deeply, even though I had done nothing wrong. Through their lens they appeared to laugh and scorn someone working in the office with no engineering degree. From that point, I felt I had to work harder than anyone to prove my place in that office. Steve, the director, had taken a punt. He had employed someone – the only person without an engineering qualification to their name, apart from the receptionist and office manager. Later he was to tell me that it had altered how he viewed someone's CV. My initial two-hour meeting with him was thanks to a colleague I worked with when I was in the RAF. Their consultancy had worked with us and I loved their work ethic. When it became obvious that I couldn't work in Cambridge, he put in a good word for me in the Bristol office and I offered to work for five weeks for free. I wasn't greedy – I was being paid resettlement money by the RAF – and I knew he wasn't convinced. However, after three weeks of working with him he sidled up to me and said: "Do you want a job?" On my CV alone he wouldn't have employed me, he said, but seeing the way I worked proved I was capable. If only we could all have that chance in employment.

Nevertheless, the experience of my colleagues with their snide comments and personal views cut me to the core. Later, one of those people actually admitted that he had been wrong; he saw I was capable and was sorry. By then though the damage had been done. One comment made in my workplace had put all my motivation for working hard into overdrive mode as I overcompensated to prove myself.

I was then seconded onto a joint venture in the public sector for two years. This is where things unravelled. The job was great, although I found it difficult to gain respect for the work I did. No one cared about my background or my skill set; actually, one person did take the time to read my CV and remarked that I should have been in a more senior role because of my skills, but he was ignored. I was just assigned jobs, with the assumption that I could do them. For the most part that was true; I had a background in the military, where you were thrown in at the deep end and you learned to cope, even if it was stressful. But two things created the pressure-cooker environment within me. The first was leading a lean project to save money and time across projects. I was told I had to be successful to have a job! No pressure, then! This was new territory for me. I had never been involved with lean projects before and no training was offered, so I had to learn new skills amid the pressure of having no long-term job. But once again, Michelle grits her teeth and throws herself into the project. I didn't dare challenge anyone or show any weakness; I felt that if I did I would either look like a failure or, worse, like my dad. Hindsight is a wonderful thing, because I think if I had used the practice of looking at myself from a third-person perspective or imagined I was giving advice to a friend with the same problem, it might have helped me find an alternative approach and a way to tackle my fears. After all, this response was based in trauma, and that needed to be worked through.

Secondly, when it came to rebidding for the contract I was put on the bid team, working long hours and under pressure. There was no guarantee I'd have a job going forward if we lost. I really had no idea if I was OK to go back to the Bristol office or not. During this time and, I believe, as a direct result of this (on top of the existing demands of single parenthood), I was plagued with fatigue and indigestion; so, taking shares out with Gaviscon, I devoured its Advance pills, until someone pointed me in the direction of Zantac. Eureka! It worked. But, treating the symptom rather than the cause, I could often be seen emailing bid documents late at night when other colleagues were, sensibly, not even switching on their computers. For some reason I felt I had to do that in order to be seen as diligent. I didn't consider that I might perform better if I was rested. I'd go home, look after the boys and start work again once they had gone to bed. This was my pace of life for about ten months. And don't even start on maintaining a personal relationship and exercise! I regularly drove up to see my partner on Friday evenings after work every fortnight, when the boys were with their dad. A drive that could take anywhere between three to five hours, depending on traffic, then the same return trip on Sunday, only to start the whole cycle again on Monday. I had no time off for me at all.

Relentless. Even holidays weren't relaxing. As a single parent, you have to be on your toes all the time. One time in Johannesburg Josh, who was five or six, went straight into a lift, thinking we were right behind. It was only when I saw his face as the door closed that I realised. A few frantic moments later, after I had initially run up the stairs to beat the lift, I saw him back down on the ground floor, grinning as though it was a mere game. Driving and catching the ferry down to the Vendée and staying at Eurocamp ended up being one of the most relaxing holidays we ever had, but the stress of navigating and working out everything myself (pre-satnav) gave me such severe indigestion that my first visit when we arrived was to a pharmacy. In Disneyworld, giving the kids the time of their life, I contracted food poisoning from one of the buffets. I couldn't eat for a week after that, but as far as the boys were concerned they were not really that aware. We had a few days near the pool where they had games afternoons, and as we were there for three weeks it didn't spoil it too much. But I do remember reaching out to one of the pool staff and asking if he could keep an eye on my kids as I was poorly. He refused, and I could have cried. Later on, though, he came up and apologised because he hadn't realised I was a single parent; I guess the kids must have told him that during the afternoon. It was lovely that he did so, but I never forgot that I felt like the world was on my shoulders.

So how does that relate to work? Well, I saw my role as a parent as another full-time job. Balancing school activities – such as fancy dress occasions, when I was magically supposed to create the most feckin' fantastic costume at a moment's notice because my little darlings had stuffed the letter in their bag until the day before – became my norm; the requirement to make cakes at 10pm the night before they were needed (those pesky notes seemed to have a life of their own) resulted in me trying to work out if I really could stay up until 11pm to make chocolate muffins or whether a tray bake from the Co-op was acceptable and could be bought in the morning. Guess which option I went for? I attended every single parents' evening for each of my boys, which didn't give me any solid feedback other than that they were doing well or they needed to pay attention more. It also required the dexterity of a ninja to move from building to building to meet the five-minute appointment time. Of course, by the time you got there, the family with a million questions and the child from hell meant that the time slot was blown out of the window anyway. There were the myriad medical appointments: asthma, eczema, vaccinations, illnesses – particularly when Matt was diagnosed with epilepsy. I was there for them every time and then made up the work time I had lost. But I approached it with military precision. I planned them all out in the calendar so I didn't miss a thing.

When both boys were in secondary school, and au pairs were not really needed, I did everything around the house. So I now had full-time work, parenthood and all the domestics. For some reason I resisted a cleaner, as that somehow – and ridiculously, now I look back – felt like I was a failure for not being able to clean my own house. My mum had managed it, so why couldn't I? Well, hello! Mum didn't work for the majority of the time, so had all that time to look after me (guffaw) and do the domestics. Quite why I thought I could be Superwoman with no impact on my physical and mental health was beyond me. I didn't even question it; as a single parent, it seemed obvious that everything should fall to me. I put pressure on myself, and again wanted to be respected for doing a lot and doing it well. However, many women married or living with someone appear to suffer the same issues. Insights gained from surveys undertaken by Deloitte show that less than 31% of women consider they have a good work–life balance, down from two-thirds pre-pandemic, and they attribute this to undertaking the majority of childcare and household tasks in addition to working. It seems we have a long way to go in societal balance when it comes to child-rearing and women in the workplace.

Even now, when I consider what I did I think that seems a hell of a lot, and also there are women in marriages or partnerships who work and still do all of these activities. I'm not belittling men. I'm suggesting we should put our own boundaries in place and share the burden equally.

I thought I could do everything alone – that I didn't need support. How wrong was I? Even if I had a family to ask for help, I suspect my pride would have stuck in my throat before I had uttered the words 'please could you do x, y or z?' I was brought up to be independent, to work things out for myself, and my experiences taught me you could rely on no one except yourself.

During my counselling sessions, my therapist said: "Michelle, everyone needs support at some point in their lives – it's not a failing and not a sign of weakness." I felt the impact of her words. It still took me a while to ask for help after that, but what I realised was that if someone asked me for help, I loved giving it. I knew I was helping them, and that meant a lot to me and the other person. So I imagined being in the other person's shoes, knowing that they felt useful in some way but didn't want to ask in case they had read the situation wrong or just didn't know how to say it. I remember losing my temper with my boys because I had too many things to do (grass cutting, tidying, cleaning, cooking) and my eldest said: "Instead of getting annoyed, why don't you just ask us to help?" Now, I say this with a grin because normally when I ask my youngest, who is eighteen, to do something, I usually get the answer "Maybe." I can't live with 'maybe', although it sometimes means 'yes' but in his time frame, not mine. This means I could often hear him smashing out the recycling in our street at 11.30pm because he had only just remembered. But Matt had a point. Instead of storing up all those things in my own head that needed doing, because I thought it was my responsibility, and then getting angry because no one could mind-read, why didn't I share what I was thinking? Well, sometimes I don't want to always have to ask. I want other people to make their minds up about what might need to be done, and do it.

As I sit here now, with both boys at university and just my friendly mutt by my side, I reflect in wonder that the house is so tidy and so damn quiet. Now I seem to have more time than ever to relax, reflect, manage my domestics and exercise. As I look back, I wish I had taken things a little slower. I doubt the result would have been much different, but going slower, taking time to rest, not thrashing myself in the gym or spending time on faddy diets, all on top of a full-time role, might have prevented my breakdown and perhaps my current neurological issues. Who knows? It's pointless wondering. Now I spend my time asking others if they really need to be Wonder Woman or Superman and if there just might be an alternative to the way they live. If only we could see into the future when we were twenty, I wonder what we would have chosen for ourselves then.

What might this mean for you?

- How afraid of failure are you? How much does it drive you to succeed? If you could operate in a different way, how would you prefer to feel instead?

- How much are you juggling the demands of daily life on top of a full-time job? Given a choice, what would you do instead?

- What steps can you take to make life easier for you and others around you?

- On a scale of 1–10 (1 being 'hardly any' and 10 being 'loads'), how much fun do you have at work and in your personal life? If you wanted to increase the score, what would you do instead?

Chapter 9

Humpty Dumpty Fell off the Wall

Down, down, down she goes,
Wherever she is going, no one knows
But hitting the bottom hurt like hell
Like landing at the bottom of an old stone well

But wait, there are steps carved into the side
They can't be seen easily, but like all things that hide
It's important to see things from a different point of view
To gain a different outcome, a life with a different hue

Michelle Ensuque

Even when I had reached rock bottom, I could feel my hand scrabbling and searching the seabed for something solid to hold on to. Something to keep me in this life and not send me to the next. I have alluded to the fact I used to think of each day as a new day when I was a child. It was a coping strategy, but a useful one – I channelled what little energy I had left and coupled it with grim bloody determination to aid my recovery. But how did I know I had reached rock bottom in the first place? Well, I'm not sure I did at the time, but someone helped me to realise.

Christmas in our house when I was growing up was lovely. There is no catch here. It was the one time of the year when an effort was made. There were presents under the (very small, artificial) tree; decorations appeared overnight on Christmas Eve; and there was a lovely roast that Mum poured her heart and soul into. Even now the timing of food for a roast is something that occasionally escapes me, and I usually forget something, but she managed to get everything on the table, all hot and steamy. It was the one time when issues were put aside, apart from when my dad bought my mum a Tefal deep fat fryer one Christmas. Mum was very displeased and I swear it could have become his head garment instead of the flimsy paper one that adorned it from the Christmas cracker. The arguments and silence that ensued led me to be in tears at the window when Father Christmas went past on his sleigh as he visited the neighbourhood. I put my hand on the glass looking out, and the rain down the window matched my tears. But they were normally happy occasions. We always played Monopoly in the evening, and a kind of invisible truce was declared.

December 2012 in my house. I remember it well. It was a cold day between Christmas and New Year, and the boys had asked if we could take Max, our dog, for a walk on the beach, and go for a meal at a pub. It was because they wouldn't be with me on my birthday, as they were spending the new year with their dad and wanted to celebrate with me early. As we woke that morning and I went to get the boys ready, while my then-partner snoozed away in bed, I could feel I was feeling overwhelmed already. What should have been a pleasant day was seemingly overshadowed by the effort of doing simple tasks, and the feeling of tears looming under the surface was ever-present. The feeling of being resentful because my partner was able to sleep. Goddammit, this was supposed to a nice time. It was Christmas! In truth, I prefer the anticipation of Christmas rather than the event itself, but I guess that's because I never imagined Christmases being like this.

Still, eventually we were ready, and we piled into the car to go. Halfway down the motorway the kids started arguing. I was tired already.

"If you keep bickering, I'm going to turn the car round and go home," I said through gritted teeth. I was tired of dealing with the fighting, shouting and crying. Then, having looked out of the windscreen at the heavy clouds and spots of rain, I looked in the rear-view mirror and asked: "Did you guys pick up your coats?" You can guess the answer. Then the boys started arguing again. My whole body went into slow motion. I had forgotten the coats. They had forgotten their coats. The day was not the day I wanted. I didn't want to walk in the freezing cold. I wanted to lie in bed, tucked up under the duvet. Without saying a word, I clicked the indicator and turned off the motorway, not towards our destination but back towards home. The car fell silent.

"Why are we going this way?" one of the boys asked.

"Because you are arguing, you have no coats and it's raining." I must have sounded weird, because no one argued. Tears streamed silently down my face.

Once back at home, I told the boys to go upstairs and I sat on the sofa. I told my partner to leave. I didn't want him in the house. I didn't want someone asking a million questions or trying to cheer me up. I just wanted some peace and to be alone. I was very calm and eerily quiet. No shouting. Just voiced what

I wanted. I think I sounded flat. Yes, that's about right. Flat and tired. My partner left. The boys were upstairs. I fed them their supper in the kitchen, but I stayed in the lounge while they were eating – the first time ever I had done this. They ate in silence. How horrible that must have been for them, but I didn't have the energy to contemplate; I was spent.

The next day, the boys left to be with their dad and I spent at least four or five days just sitting on the sofa, looking out of the window, watching mindless TV. I felt like I had folded in on myself, like a balloon that had lost all its air. Then one day, as I was on Facebook, I was messaging a friend. Gently she asked: "Could you have depression?" I thought, *Maybe, but honestly I've no idea.* I found myself looking on the Internet for symptoms, and was horrified to find out that I was experiencing the majority of them.

The next day, I booked a doctor's appointment. For me, depression was something that happened to other people, and when it did I imagined it was some significant event, not what I was experiencing.

I remember making the doctor's appointment. In fact, I made two. The first time, I phoned the receptionist and just booked an appointment for mid-January. It didn't seem like a big deal; I felt a bit of a fraud and wasn't actually sure what I was going to say.

Just as the new year started, I went back to work. That was hard. It felt like I was wading through treacle. Everything seemed slow, hard work; I felt heavy and low in mood. I could appear normal to the outside world, though, able to have a laugh and converse with some energy. But as soon as I turned around, the curtain came down on my face. That pretence took it out of me, and once I got home I was just able to manage the basics and then I'd haul myself under the covers to sleep.

I kept going like that for about three days, and then suddenly a phone call changed everything and I slid into the abyss. I had a call from someone talking about my ex-husband, and it wasn't an area I wanted to visit. My ex-husband was my ex – and had been, by that time, for quite a few years. The last thing I wanted to be reminded of was the impact that relationship had had on me. Once the call was over I felt crushed, tired. I had taken the call in a meeting room and, as I looked outside the glass door at everyone going about their business, I felt claustrophobic, trapped in a box, and I had no idea how I was going to get out.

In desperation I phoned the doctor's surgery to see if I could move my appointment, and I don't know how but I ended up talking to the on-call doctor, who ran through a few questions. As she asked me various things, I remember crying and literally sliding down the wall.

She gently asked: "Could you come in now?"

I managed to whimper "Yes" and pulled myself together. I've no idea what excuse I gave to leave work – it's all a blur – but I left immediately and found myself at the surgery (I don't remember the drive). There I went through another list of questions, including whether I had suicidal thoughts. At least that one I could answer "No" to. Prozac was prescribed, and although I'd heard of it, I didn't really know what it was. I felt a mixture of relief and shame. Shame, because I never thought I would be on antidepressants: they were for people who couldn't cope, and up until that point I was one of life's copers. Relief, because I had nothing else left to give, and I stuck my hand out for my prescription, like a kid expecting sweeties. My coping strategies and strength had left me, leaving me bare and exposed to everything life had thrown at me, and all I could rely on was a little magic pill.

The doctor asked me what I wanted to do about work. My first thought was: *They can't know.* So I elected not to be signed off. The doctor said she thought it was a good idea, as I would have less time to "wallow" and work would offer some sort of distraction. I think she was right; I know some people simply must take time off to rest and recuperate, but I couldn't. The shame of admitting to my colleagues that I couldn't cope – during a time when I wasn't even sure if I had a job, going forward – was not something I could contemplate. So, after that appointment, I picked up my pills and went straight back to work. No one could know.

Looking at the pill packet later, I wondered what was going to happen when I took them. What effect would they have on me? How would I feel? It's the reason I've never taken psychedelic drugs – I was too scared of what impact they might have. Could people tell I was on them? I mean, how ridiculous is that? How would anyone actually know just by looking at me? It wasn't as if I was wearing a placard that said 'Useless person, on drugs to get better'. But nothing about this made any sense, and it's what I thought.

What helped was my friend and neighbour, a nurse, who told me many people used them, and said: "Michelle, think of it as a support. It's not something to feel ashamed about." That made me view them, and other people, in a new light. It made me wonder who in my network might be suffering too.

Now, don't laugh: despite being at rock bottom and having no energy, I still went to gym classes. I believed that exercise was good for you and I should make every effort to help myself. That's what we are told, isn't it? And if we don't exercise, we are lazy. I didn't last long. I soon realised that as I looked at my lifeless face in the mirror, with the feeling that my body felt like a concrete block, I saw the class simply as something to get through. After a few weeks, I abandoned it in favour of concentrating on the things that actually needed to be done, and prioritised rest instead. There was, I thought, plenty of time for exercise later.

Six weeks later I noticed a change. I was driving to work and started humming to the tunes on the radio. I stopped and smiled. When was the last time I had done that? I always used to hum. In fact, the lack of doing that now, especially when driving, is a sign or a trigger that I need to throttle back on life. It's a simple check. Understanding and looking out for those triggers means I constantly check in with myself to make sure I am OK. Now I listen to my mind (especially the self-talk) instead of ignoring it, and take heed of how my body is feeling. So that was the start of feeling better, but my eventual recovery was to take over a year of self-reflection, hard work and a better understanding of me before I was done.

Now, it is only when I look back that I realise that it also took at least a year to bring me to my knees. A year, following my father's death and dealing with my stepmother and the wranglings of his estate, and receiving the smallest of boxes of all my parents' possessions. A year when I continued to work and, to be honest, just thought that life was a little 'meh'. I thought it must be like this for everyone. But it wasn't just that year. It was all of those years. My childhood, my abuse, my lack of fulfilment, my drive to succeed, my failed relationships, my personal drivers and coping strategies led me to this place. They came crashing down around my ears.

The other thing I realise when I look back is my utterly insane (I can say this now, but at the time it seemed to make complete sense) approach to diet and exercise as I sought perfection. The trouble was I could never recognise when I had achieved it…well, in my mind I never did, so I kept chasing an ideal. My dad had wanted someone 'pretty' like his goddaughter. I was never going to look like her; but in my attempt at becoming a pretty version of her, I denied myself certain nutrients and constantly exercised, on top of the stressful lifestyle I was leading. I think this was also a big factor in my eventual depressed state.

My research has led me to realise I might have unwittingly created a situation where my body was not able to function properly or defend itself in the face of an unknown onslaught such as a virus. My current neurological condition, which sees me with pain in my calves (like a gnawing toothache), with constant pins and needles in my feet and with muscle fasciculations all over my body, might well be as a result of the demyelination of my spinal cord and/or stress. The former may well have been caused by a virus leaving its mark on my poor, defenceless immune system (there is certainly a mark or a lesion on my spine). Who knows? But the way I was living certainly didn't help my situation. Life certainly has to be at a slower pace now, as I am unable to exercise like I used to. Running has been replaced by walking. The dog is not complaining, although he'd probably prefer to go longer than my 4–5km maximum distance. As far as I am aware though, he does not lie awake in agony after a longer walk, unable to sleep.

If only I had known these things earlier in life, I wouldn't have gone on strict, low-fat diets…or any kind of diet, in fact. I would have just eaten, with nutrition first and foremost at the back of my mind. Eating to ensure my body and mind could be the strongest it could be. Don't get me wrong: I wasn't eating loads of processed foods; I cooked from scratch and felt quite smug, in that takeaways were a rare event. But for long periods I would deny myself certain nutrients, follow the latest trend and exercise far too much.

If I had known these things earlier in life, I would have been kinder on my body. I would have rested appropriately after being ill instead of racing back to the gym, only to find myself sicker and unable to exercise for even longer.

If only we had a crystal ball to see into a future that is the culmination of the choices we make. But, as much as all the things I listed brought me to my knees, some of those things – such as grit, determination, hard work, self-reflection and the art of seeing every day as a new day – also brought about my recovery.

What might this mean for you?

- Look at your life over the past year and write down the highs and lows. What does that look like to you? Does the balance need to be redressed?

- What is your belief about mental health? What have you been taught about it? How do you feel about others who suffer mental health issues, either at work or personally?

- If you have suffered or are suffering, what help have you sought, or what help might you seek if you haven't already done so?

- What targets can you focus on to help you enjoy your life more?

Chapter 10

My Knight in Shining Armour

No, not my husband, although he came a pretty close second. He was, I think, a result of my first saviour: NLP.

I don't believe in coincidences. I've had too many of them. I tend to think of them as choices. Things are put in our path for us to choose and it is up to us to decide which path to take. It's just my view. One of those moments was when I was introduced to NLP. I was at dinner with friends and one of the ladies, Nicky, was an NLP coach. I had never heard of NLP and had never even considered any type of coaching until that point. I was intrigued when she said she could determine what was going on with someone when they walked into her coaching practice. It wasn't 'just' coaching in her case that made her special, it was her intuition that enabled her to get to the nub of the problem quickly.

I'd been going to counselling for about a year and, while it was helpful to unburden myself with someone, I was getting bored of the sound of my own voice and the same story I was telling. I've never been the type of person who looks backwards, so I wanted something to propel me into the future on a different course. Something that would change the way

I thought; less of a victim, more a sassy in-control bitch. OK, not bitch exactly, but you know what I mean; something akin to Scarlett Johansson from the Avengers. A kick-ass kind of gal.

After talking to Nicky, I decided to give it a whirl. After all, this was an opportunity that I had not explored before. What did I have to lose?

It turned out to be an amazing opportunity that changed my life. It changed me as a person, colleague, parent, friend and partner, as well as changing my career path. Compared to attending counselling every week for nearly a year, I had four sessions. That's it. I experienced shifts in how I thought, both during the session and afterwards, and I have *never* returned to how I used to think and behave.

NLP gave me the ability to enter my subconscious in a deep and hitherto unthought-of way. I am way too much of a coward to use something like psychedelic drugs, for fear of either not being in control or what it might do to my body and mind, now or in the long term. Instead, when I entered into this state I knew what was real and what was not. Images would pop up like mini-movies and I could tap into feelings and thoughts I was previously unaware of. Just like my dream at the start of this book, I found I could change the colour of the movie, the speed and the sounds, and I could reverse it, fast-forward it or slow it down, all with my mind.

So what is NLP and how does it work? It was developed in the 1970s, about the same time that cognitive behavioural therapy (CBT) made its entrance. It was developed by Dr Richard Bandler and John Grinder, and is about making changes at the unconscious level. They observed sessions by psychotherapists such as Fritz Perls, Virginia Satir and Milton Erickson, identifying common patterns and positive suggestions that they used to help their clients change. Once they had identified these patterns, Bandler and Grinder applied them in their own sessions and reproduced similar results. This was the start of NLP, which offers a toolkit of techniques and a mindset based on the study of human excellence. If a client doesn't resonate with one technique, a different one can be used to bring about the desired change. Each treatment is tailored to the client, and no two treatments are exactly the same.

Think about undertaking a task for the first time; for many of us a good example is learning to drive. When we first start lessons, we must think of those tasks consciously. Everything feels slow, cumbersome and awkward, so we practise until the process becomes so ingrained that sometimes we can drive from A to B without even remembering the journey or the actions that enabled us to get there safely. That's when the process has gone into our subconscious thought. A lot of our patterns of behaviour stem from repetition, but it can also be one event that triggers a pattern of thought for us that we repeat to protect ourselves. For example, if a child is humiliated by a teacher at school (it happened a few times at my school), that same child might become withdrawn in future and not ask so many questions, for fear of being ridiculed. That might be fine in a school context, but fast-forward ten or more years, when they are in a work environment. Here they may be accused of not being willing to take on responsibility or of lacking commitment, which might affect their promotion and advancement opportunities. When patterns of behaviour work for us it's great, but when they have outlived their usefulness or are inflexible to new situations, that's when we can become stuck.

I remember my first session clearly. Nicky had said: "Leave plenty of time to find parking." I duly did, or thought I had.

Her house was only four miles away from mine and I knew the area well. I had factored in forty-five minutes to drive and park – plenty of time, but it was as though everything was against me that day. Roadworks and slow drivers (my road rage was at its worst) delayed me by probably a whopping five minutes, but it felt like thirty. The parking situation was, to put it bluntly, a shitstorm. Everywhere was rammed. It was either permit-only parking or I had to park much further away and walk/run to her place. I was fuming and shouting in my car. Anyone watching would have thought I'd either lost the plot or was shouting at someone on the hands-free phone. I was apoplectic.

The final straw was trying to turn up a road for about the fifth time only to be confronted by a JCB in the middle of the road. I felt like I was going to explode or have a heart attack, I had got myself so worked up; I hate being late. I'd much rather be two hours early than five minutes late, but of course that increases the pressure. Swearing profusely, I reversed and drove up another road towards Nicky's and, as if by magic, a space appeared just outside her house. I had five minutes to spare. I parked, then walked into her apartment as though nothing had happened. In asking me what I wanted to concentrate on that day, it was easy: to reduce the anxiety and anger in me that raged like the Running of the Bulls festival in Pamplona. The only difference was that there was no risk of death by the end of it, but physically and mentally I was exhausted with the self-torture and corralling of emotions to one or two points in my body – my stomach and/or my chest. But the questioning was about to get interesting…

"So explain to me how the anxiety and anger shows up," Nicky said. That was easy. I just had to regale the previous forty-five minutes. In hindsight it seemed hilarious, almost out of a comedy sketch, but it was anything but hilarious to me.

"And if you weren't anxious and angry, how would you want to feel?" she asked.

These questions were way too easy. I answered: "Relaxed, calm, in control."

"So just take me through, in slow motion, what was going on for you in the lead-up to coming here?"

I slowed it down and went through it step by step. The wish to not be late. The despair about the roadworks and lack of parking, and that whatever road I tried to go up, there was something preventing me. But more specifically, I said: "So it's like there is a voice one side of my head that says, 'You will be fine. You left loads of time and there is no need to worry, you've done your best.' Immediately, the other voice jumps in and responds, 'Yes, but look at the traffic. You will never find a place to park and you will be late, and what will that look like?' Then the other voice tries to calm me down: 'No, it's fine, you've still got twenty minutes to find somewhere.' But the other voice starts snarling, 'See? Told you that you wouldn't find a car park space.' The other voice responds, 'It's OK, you will be OK, honestly.' It tries to tell me it doesn't matter, that it is sure Nicky will understand, but the other voice butts in, shouting, 'No! It won't be OK, you'll run out of time. Useless. I told you!' Then silence. As soon as I found a car park space, the voices stopped."

"Whose voices do you think you hear?" Nicky asked gently.

I wasn't expecting that, and was starting to think she would think I was a bit cuckoo and perhaps in need of some serious psychotherapy. I mean, I could hear voices!

"Um, well, one is definitely mine – the soothing one, the one trying to keep me calm."

"And the other?"

"My dad." Woah, how did those words slip out of my mouth? I mean, up until that precise moment, I had just thought it was me thinking those thoughts. Just me. No one else here, folks! But as soon as I said it, I knew it was right. His voice, barking orders, making me jump or stand to attention, making me feel I had let other people down or was simply stupid. After all, how many times had I heard him say I lacked common sense?

"And what would you like to do to that voice?"

"Eh? You mean there are choices? I can have some control over it? OK, I'd like to put some Sellotape over his mouth." I giggled. It felt naughty, and I swear it was the first thing I thought of. The golden rule of NLP is that the first thought is often your subconscious one. The one that appears with no effort whatsoever, no matter how random.

Now one voice was silent, and we started to do something else – we were only about fifteen minutes into the session at this stage – when suddenly I stopped and said: "Sorry, all I can see is my dad's face trying to talk behind the Sellotape. It's going to have to go."

"So what would you like to do with it?"

"I'd like it to slide off the edge of the world, like the sun disappears at sunset." I was getting used to this now. I had relaxed. In my mind I could see the image slip down and down until I could no longer see it, and we carried on with the rest of the session.

I walked out of her house as light as a feather for the first time in many, many years. My head was silent. No arguing. No negative, barking comments. Nothing. I cannot tell you how that felt. It felt like I had been released from a prison – the prison in my mind, at least. I have never, to this day, had that voice return in my head. Not once.

Years later I was to come across a lady named Dr Edith Eger, an Auschwitz survivor who explained how she chose to see her guards as the real prisoners, turned hate into pity and described her horrific experience as an "opportunity". In NLP terms this is known as reframing: taking a situation that seems negative and looking at it from a different perspective. She believes, as I do, that we have the power to free ourselves from the prisons of our own minds.

Now, NLP works on many levels, and I find it easy to visualise. Others might work more on a feelings or auditory level, and that's OK too. A good coach determines the best way to connect with a person and then helps them free themselves from the beliefs that can hold them back. Four sessions were all it took for me to see things from a different angle, change my beliefs about myself, stop criticising myself so much and see a future for myself, as opposed to a short life with sadness as an overriding memory.

I was so blown away with the results that I trained as an NLP coach, and from the same training establishment as Nicky, through John Seymour (who learned from the founders of NLP) and more recently his protégé, Neil Arnold from 91 Untold. I was dumbfounded by the fact that I could think in a completely different way from before and be unable to return to my old self. The training enabled me to understand myself better and gave me tools and techniques to not only use with individual clients and in my consultancy work but also put into practice in my own life. Gone are the days when I took people at face value. Now I take time to consider what might be going on for them. What belief systems they are running. What stories they might be telling themselves. Fundamentally, I have learned to connect with them as fellow human beings.

In fact, one of the training sessions turned out to be as fundamental as that 'voice in the head' session I had previously experienced. Our trainer, Neil, conducted demonstrations with volunteers and would then take feedback and questions after the session. I won't give the specific details of the exercise we were doing, for personal reasons, but suffice to say it boiled down to how I operated as an individual and the effect of other people's behaviour on me. I had suggested that someone else I knew needed to learn how to let people into their world. I was immediately asked: "When did you last let someone in?" I was floored. Since when was this about me? Wasn't it about the other person? I remember my expression at that time. Utter confusion, and I felt my mind grasping for the answer in my head and failing. The confusion was also because I thought of myself as an empathetic individual. Always ready to listen to someone else and being sympathetic. Surely that meant I was open and let people in, didn't I? Hmm, that was proving difficult to remember.

I said: "I know I should tell you that it's my partner, but I am not sure that is totally true." That felt weird to say, because I have felt a greater connection with Alain than with anyone else in my entire life.

"So what about pets?" Neil asked.

"No, definitely not. If you let them in, they die." Curious that I had thought that, because I had never had a pet until recent years, never mind one that had died on me.

"OK, can you imagine what it would be like to let someone in?" Neil asked.

The only thing I could come up with was a movie. I'd just watched *Pretty Woman* for the umpteenth time and saw what it was like for two people to have a glimpse inside each other's worlds.

So I gave that as my example. The demo continued (there was a lot more to it than that) and we sat down to get feedback and take questions. But I was dumbfounded. I didn't hear what anyone was saying. I had realised, in that session, I had never opened up sufficiently to let anyone in. Probably for fear of rejection, or as a self-protection strategy. It didn't really matter why; the real issue was that now I knew that, I couldn't unknow it. I remember telling Alain about the exercise and he looked at me and said: "Fuck, I thought you had let me in. Imagine what it will be like now if you do!" Anyone who hears him say 'fuck' in a sexy French accent and with his wry sense of humour will understand why we both laughed our heads off. But in all seriousness, I then opened up to him about things that were personal and painful to me, and in that space we have continued to do that for each other, each giving the other a safe space in which to share our innermost thoughts.

As I mentioned, NLP changed me. I am more measured in my responses, rather than jumping to conclusions, more prompting than seeking solutions and more consultative than decisive.

NLP's critics refer to the lack of 'research' that proves it works. Sturt et al. conclude: "There is little evidence that NLP interventions improve health-related outcomes. This conclusion reflects the limited quantity and quality of NLP research, rather than robust evidence of no effect. There is currently insufficient evidence to support the allocation of NHS resources to NLP activities outside of research purposes."[1]

---

1.   Sturt J. et al. (2013) 'Neurolinguistic programming: A systematic review of the effects on health outcomes'.

However, a more recent paper[2] is far more favourable, concluding: "Neuro-Linguistic Psychotherapy as a psychotherapeutic modality grounded in theoretical frameworks, methodologies and interventions scientifically developed, including models developed by NLP, shows results that can hold its ground in comparison with other psychotherapeutic methods."

I can categorically say it worked for me and it has worked for countless other people whom I have since seen as clients. Nothing gives me more joy than seeing the utter look of disbelief on their face when they have their own light-bulb moment and go away much more light-hearted. One client summed their experience up much better than I could: "CBT taught me that if I kept putting my hand on the lamp, I wouldn't feel the heat. NLP took the lamp away."

That person in particular has changed every aspect of their lives – how they approach their work, being able to travel without extreme anxiety preventing them venturing far from the house, improving their marriage and also improving their relationship with their child.

There is also some nuance here; you have to genuinely want to change. You might have to believe it will work, although in my case I had absolutely no idea whether it would or wouldn't, as I'd never heard of it, but I went in open-minded as to its possibilities. It depends whether you have rapport in the relationship between client and coach. If it is lacking, I would suggest trying a different coach rather than dismissing NLP altogether. And finally, something else might work better for

---

2.   Zaharia C., Reiner M. and Schütz P. (2015) 'Evidence-based Neuro Linguistic Psychotherapy; a meta-analysis'.

you and that is fine. We are all different, and I am not one to force anyone to have NLP if they think that hypnotherapy (again, subconscious-based) or something on a more conscious, practical level, such as CBT, might be a better fit. But in words from the NLP world: 'If what you are doing isn't working, try *anything* else.'

> **What might this mean for you?**
>
> - If you have never heard of NLP and are now interested, my first suggestion would be contacting the Association for NLP (www.anlp.org), as the coaches following their programme have studied for hundreds of hours and have gained the accreditation needed. In an area where coaching is unregulated, it's a good place to start.
>
> - What other therapies could you try if you don't like the thought of NLP but still want to change?
>
> - What in this chapter has made you think: *That's what I do*?

Chapter 11

Choice

My journey and research into the many factors that might result in depression or other mental health issues highlights how people might be affected by their past, which might thus 'show up' in life. Examples are:

1. lack of confidence, which cripples one's ability to progress at work, carry out public speaking, talk to bosses about salary increases, or try new things
2. lack of self-belief that they can achieve their ambitions
3. relationship issues
4. conflict and fear of conflict
5. low self-esteem, leading to unhappiness with jobs and body image.

When we are robbed of our self-esteem by people who purport to love us, it leaves an indelible mark. We can choose to be defined by those moments or we can choose to define our life the way we want it ourselves. I was angry for the childhood I had lost and the tortured adult I became, but I realised, since both of my parents were dead, that the only person I was really hurting was me. I owed it to myself to find my own happiness, inside and out. To do that, I had to make a choice.

As I look back on my life, I realise I made choices either because I had reached a stage where continuing along my trajectory just wasn't acceptable or sustainable any more or because opportunities presented themselves. I have also made choices not to do something because to make the change would have been discordant with what was important to me.

I chose to leave my parents' home at about the age of seventeen. I could not take any more, and moved in with my piano teacher and his family in my home town. They had offered me their attic room for £10 a week including food, and with my part-time job earnings this was doable. They were so lovely, and it was nice to be in a stress-free environment for once in my life. Packing all my belongings felt final and sad, because the irony for many who suffer abuse is that it is all they have known. An unsafe environment but home nonetheless. The unknown world was one full of promise but unexplored, so it was a risk, a leap of faith that it would be a new dawn. After a few weeks my nan died, and shortly before she did I visited her in hospital. My parents were there. My mum's lips were pursed together as if they had been sewn into a line from the inside, and my dad simply said: "Can we have the key back to the house, please?" That was it. I wasn't sure what I was expecting, but for a long time I think I lived in hope they would realise what they had done and somehow beg for forgiveness. But no, that was the start of me realising that to change my future, I had to change my present. It meant I was really poor for a long time after that and, during some particularly bad periods, had to live hand to mouth on £10 a week for food; basically, a chicken and basics was my weekly shop. I was often in tears when another bill landed, and I was in debt. But I never gave up; to give up was giving up on me.

I chose to give up music and change careers. I never wanted to be a musician. Not really. I was good at it, but it didn't make my heart soar. What I wanted to be was a psychologist, but psychology had only just started as a subject and I was dissuaded. I learned the hard way that listening to others and bending to their view usually ended up in disappointment, and that listening to my intuition instead led to happiness. I applied to the RAF, where I was told to go away for two years, do something different and come back. So I gave up music, moved to London, went into catering, and funded myself through night school to do bookkeeping and accounts. Again I was on the breadline, but I did feel I was making progress. By the time two years were up, I was a much more well-rounded individual, and when I reapplied, two years to the day from the first application, I was successful.

I chose not to abuse my children. That was the biggest and most important decision I have ever made. It was also the hardest. Not in terms of making it, but carrying through with it every day, until not abusing them was part of my subconscious. I've covered the details of that previously, but I had worried about being a mother myself for many years. I had avoided it, for fear of turning out like both of my parents. Voicing it, rather than just saying it in my head, and making it a real commitment not to be like them helped me make a commitment to myself, I think, to follow through.

I chose not to go self-employed when the boys were younger, even when given the opportunity that might well have netted me a small fortune by my standards, but I knew it meant time on the road. I had also realised during my NLP training that my top values were money and love (primarily for my boys), followed by health. (How often do we even think of such things?) I felt shocked when I couldn't separate my top values: love and money. When I dug down deeper, I realised the money value was attached to security, which was attached to keeping a roof over my children's heads, so it wasn't about having money to show I had money – there was a real reason behind it. I chose being there for my children because being in full-time employment, rather than in the risky world of contracting, provided me with the security needed. Choices aren't always about personal advancement – they are sometimes about what is right at a particular time in our lives.

I chose to set my own boundaries. That was a big one. I had been messed about by men – or rather, I had allowed myself to be messed about by them. My supposed role model was someone who detested the way I looked, never seemed to be proud (he did grudgingly say he was proud when I graduated to the RAF), and used me as a punchbag. It is not surprising to realise that those formative experiences set the pattern for my long-term expectations. I was treated like shit and that was how I expected to be treated. It was my norm. My mother was complicit in that she did not, or could not, do anything to change my life. When I was growing up there was no social media, no one to talk to. With no siblings, I existed in my own little world. Without any experiences to compare myself to, I believed everyone was treated like this. I didn't even realise that I was attracting people with similar traits or people who were themselves broken in some way that I had no idea how to fix. The best thing I ever did was get angry and decide what were acceptable behaviours for me. More importantly, I found my voice and spoke up when I felt hurt.

There were three events in the same month that enraged

me, and all three of them involved men: a work colleague; a close friend whom I considered a potential partner; and my ex-husband. Two events affected me personally and the third affected me and my boys, and I was as mad as hell that other people could seemingly continue to stamp over our lives as though we were incidental. I was mad that I seemed to keep falling foul of these behaviours and that these things seemed to be happening to me.

Then suddenly I stopped, and I took a long, hard look at myself and I spoke to myself as though I were speaking to a twin. "What the hell are you doing? How much longer are you going to let this continue? How does doing what you are doing help your situation, and how exactly has that worked out so far? So what are you going to do?" I actually felt myself grow taller. In fact, when I then dealt with all three of those people individually, calmly but firmly, I felt different. I wasn't an emotional wreck. I was standing up for what I believed in and what I felt was fair for me and my boys. I wasn't going to get anywhere by cowering and hoping to be rescued.

That same month I went onto Match.com, and decided that whoever I found on there would have to accept me and my boys as a package and also accept there was going to have to be some compromise, because I had the boys twenty-four-seven. When I met my future husband, I laid out the ground rules for behaviour I would *not* accept.

What is strange is that at work I didn't display any of these putting-up-with-shit traits. I was strong, confident, could make decisions and stand by them. But personally? It was the exact opposite, which goes to prove we don't really know what is going on for other people behind closed doors. When we peer into the windows of their world, we see their life through our own eyes.

I chose to recover from my depression. I'm not being

sanctimonious here. I'm not saying everyone can. I'm saying I decided. In the beginning, I was so low I wasn't even sure if it was possible. But that little voice inside me said: "Come on, you're a fighter, this is what you do, you've got to find a way." Being a fighter and a coper had an advantage after all. I chose to pay privately for counselling, although I was also lucky enough to be able to afford it; at £50 a week for nearly a year, it wasn't exactly cheap. But I shopped at charity shops for clothes and reprioritised my funds. I took the medication, the mother of all antidepressants, Prozac, and used it as a support so I could function better. I think this, combined with therapy, helped me, as I'm not sure that individually they would have been as impactful. Even the new big business I can now see looming on the horizon involving the controlled use of psychedelic drugs – which I fear may be used in isolation for people to trip into their mind, real or fantasy – should not be thought of as a quick fix. Yes, the drugs can address the symptoms, but to recover properly we need to look at the cause. After that, we must consider the part we have to play in understanding our reactions to those things that have driven us to the place we might find ourselves.

What might this mean for you?

- What choices are open to you at this very moment to change your life?
- If you were going to make one choice, to change your working life today, what would that be?
- If you were going to make one choice, to change your personal life today, what would that be?

Chapter 12

Getting your Shit Together

Oi, you! Yes, back where we started. But, hopefully, if you are reading this, you are way behind me on the steps of time. So it's like I'm in the movie *Back to the Future*, visiting you now to rewrite a potential future where pain and suffering might be lurking around the corner. OK, I'm not saying we should avoid all suffering. Some – such as the loss of a loved one, losing a job, illness – is likely to happen at some point, but it's what we do with those experiences and how we feel about them that is relevant. I'm also not saying everyone will suffer, but for some of you reading this, you might also be living a life that hasn't panned out quite as you expected, and some might have lived experiences far, far worse than mine. But you have time to reflect and act.

I'm not the type of person to look back. But let's imagine I did and that, in doing so, I could rearrange my future life for a healthier, happier me. What could I have done?

There is a limit
There is a limit to how much a person can cope with, and it

is different for everyone. As I look at my own upbringing, I assumed everyone had had the same experience as I had, and when I did talk about my experiences and discovered that that was not the case, I was shocked, but then assumed it was just because I hadn't talked to many people. I had no idea that at some point in the future I wouldn't be able to cope. So, with the benefit of hindsight, I wished I had talked to someone professionally about it. And whom would I have talked to? Well, I guess, anyone I would have felt comfortable with. I wasn't even aware of NLP then, but that isn't the only avenue, and many more therapies are either in existence today or at least there is a better awareness of them. So someone in the psychiatric sphere, a counsellor, a CBT specialist, a hypnotherapist or someone from the alternative therapy fraternity – although the term 'alternative' implies to me something that you only try once you've exhausted other avenues, which I think is a shame. In sum, look at what you have coped with and what you are going through, and ask yourself how heavy that burden feels. Don't be tempted to compare yourself to others or assume it is weak to seek support. Talk to anyone who might help.

Understand your drivers

Understanding what motivates us is key to unlocking positive and negative behaviours. Without some of my drive I might not have been so determined to succeed, so I wouldn't have wanted to remove that completely. But maybe dimming the drive switch slightly rather than applying it to every aspect of my life might have resulted in me not burning myself out. I also think it's important to understand the motivations of other people around us, because we don't just exist in our own world. Being able to communicate effectively with others is crucial, e.g. active rather than passive listening – the latter being where we are merely thinking about our point and not really listening to the other person. Our drivers are not necessarily the same as another person's, so it is easy to misunderstand each other. We are human beings who need to be connected with other human beings, and when we can't make those relationships work it can drag us down psychologically, faster than a lead weight in water.

I'd have tried to understand what made me react to things in a certain way. Why some things might have upset me that didn't upset others. Why I might be accused of taking things to heart too much.

I would suggest talking to an NLP coach or a psychologist who understands what might be driving you and who can alert you to those things, as often it is difficult to see them as problems when they are part of our make-up.

Self-reflection

I used to think I was empathetic, but now I am not so sure. I spent too much time feeling wounded and hurt to see things from other people's perspectives. For example, when my ex-husband changed jobs (and countries) to fall in line with my career or, alternatively, drove one and a half hours in each direction for work because our accommodation was in the middle of nowhere – when all I had to do was roll out of bed and walk or cycle to work on an RAF base – I didn't really think about it. I didn't put myself in his shoes. At the same time, he never really spoke about his feelings, but I am sure it increased his resentment a little bit every day each time we had to change where we lived. If I were going through that now, I'd look at how we could compromise, but I didn't see any options at that time, so I just kept quiet – for me, at least, life was easy. Sure, I thought about his situation, but he seemed happy enough, so I never pressed. We don't come out of the womb with the ability to be this perfect being. We are always a work in progress. So looking at ourselves, holding up the mirror and asking ourselves some questions might just identify some thoughts that weren't there previously.

When you experience trauma, deal with it

When we are born there are no expectations, just experiences and modelling and learned behaviour. To experience trauma when we are young is dreadful. To not feel safe with the people supposed to provide unconditional love, and yet that fear is all you've known, is something so complicated that it's much easier to ignore. As a kid, you learn to cope. What choice do you have? How do you know whether these events might lead to something much more damaging in the future? How do you know if this might even cause physical problems, because you have felt under so much stress on a daily basis that you live life like a coiled spring? How do you know you have to deal with it, when you feel that you *are* dealing with it every day?

I realised I had never dealt with my childhood or my mum's suicide. The latter was just another event, such was the life with my parents. The silence following her death was an inevitable outcome, if you will, of the shame of that experience. Silence, in the feeling that I was not good enough or worthy enough to stick around for. Silence, in that no one around us knew what to say. They stared in a sad but despairing way, but nothing came out of their mouths. The shame of it all was something to bury deep inside. Once there, it was quiet; I could ignore it and get on with life. But it was lurking in the shadows wherever I went. Even my happiest moments were tinged with the sadness of that time.

I felt I was 'in control' of my emotions, and I was proud of that. I thought I could talk openly about it, although I later realised I could only talk about it when it was on my terms. If someone asked me about it out of the blue, I would suddenly and surprisingly find myself bursting into tears. If you find yourself burying emotions in an effort to avoid dealing with them, or because you think you need to keep a stiff upper lip, my advice would be: don't! Yes, it might work for a while, even a long while, as a coping strategy but, like my view of Spanx, the holy grail to 'Bridget Jones's big pants svelte figure day', that fat has gotta come out somewhere! Yep, you might have a skinny torso, but in reality that 'extra bit' on your arse is now on the back of your neck like the Hunchback of Notre Dame.

Create boundaries

Learn to put boundaries in place for unacceptable behaviours. I didn't. I took shit from people time and time again. I was used to it. I'd almost been trained to think that was what was expected. When I did finally put boundaries in place, it was such a revelation. I almost felt naughty for doing it. But it was a real release. Others were made aware of my expectations and I felt good for making clear what was and wasn't acceptable to me.

Look after yourself

We are not superhuman. And just like the burdens, we are all different in terms of how much we can do or take on. We tend to spend our time caring for others and forget to care for ourselves. If there are things I could have done to help myself, they would have been:

- Prioritise what was important to achieve in my day, especially when I was a single parent, raising two boys and working full-time.
- Stop feeling guilty about taking time off work when I was sick.
- Stop flogging myself at the gym on a daily basis.
- Stop flogging myself at the gym after being ill, only to fall ill again and be off work for longer.
- Try not to do faddy diets. If you have specific requirements due to a condition or culture and beliefs, then do what is right for you. Whatever you do, try and eat as healthily as you can. Research the ways to eat for your own health and don't believe all the hype you see. Remember, it wasn't so long ago that we were being told that fat was bad. Then there was a massive industry built around low-fat foods, which fed nicely into my own insecurities but, in reality, were laden with sugar instead. Fast-forward twenty years and suddenly not all fat is bad and sugar has become the main culprit.
- Take some time out to recharge and rest, whatever that means to you.
- Ask questions and seek answers. For example, I used to put GPs on a pedestal but now, when we have an overstretched, failing organisation that is focused

not so much on preventative medicine as on reactive medicine, I believe in asking for answers if you aren't getting what you need. It took me twenty years and for me to finally lose my shit before I was taken seriously about examining the underlying causes for my nerve condition along with my family's history of heart disease and diabetes. I'm now seeing a cardiologist who is treating my case seriously. Don't suffer in silence, because someone, somewhere will listen. Write, phone, be a pain in the arse, because no one else apart from you is going to fight your corner.

- Be curious. Ask questions. Use Google, read books, listen to podcasts, anything. Take charge of your own life and do what is right for you. People will always try to tell you what to do. I try not to tell others, because each of us is unique, so what works for one person won't necessarily work for another. Sometimes it's just about timing. That talking therapy that you aren't ready for right now? Give it some thought and reflection, and in a few months' time you might be.

Support network

Build a support network. I was an only child and used to my own company. In truth I didn't think I needed anyone. My military career provided a ready-made support network but after that, when my friends were sporadically based around the UK and I moved to somewhere new, suddenly I found myself starting all over again. But it's not so easy. If you work full-time, you are not the primary person dropping and picking kids off at school. In addition, I was too busy to find a hobby outside of work; whether I really was too busy (normally at the gym) or simply thought I had no right for time to myself was debatable, but in either case, I didn't.

Many problems for individuals and families now stem from not having a robust support network. My family was non-existent and my husband's was on the other side of the world. Not only is it important for us to have support in our friends and colleagues network but where family exists and is able, that's important too. Grandparents can provide a welcome break from the demands of little children and, in turn, that relationship can turn into something very special.

Support networks are hugely underestimated in today's society as we chase material things. Increasingly isolated, we work harder, ignoring the demands our busy lives play on us. What if we stopped to think a little about how we could do things differently?

Ask for help

Sounds simple, but without a support network or family there was no one to ask. In reality, even when there *were* people to ask I didn't, for fear of being a burden. Yet the fact I was always there for others was not lost on me. I loved helping other people; it made me feel useful. It's only now I am happy to ask for someone else's help, because I know they get joy out of supporting me as much as I get pleasure from being relieved of a task. My husband's first line of response, when he can see I am stressed, is to ask: "How can I help?" Asking this makes me stop and reflect as to what he could actually do that would reduce my stress levels. The old me would have said "Nothing."

In fact, my mum used to say: "If a job's worth doing well, it's worth doing yourself." I disagree. I am not perfect and I don't have to do everything. Sometimes some jobs don't need doing at all, or at the very least there is another way to achieve what we need to.

Remember you have the right to choose

By and large I like to think that I have made good choices – or, at the very least, I have just made choices. The most fundamental one was not to repeat with my children the parental behaviours I endured. They deserved better, and I felt that I was in control of that. Having read *Atomic Habits* by James Clear, I followed his thought process long before that book ever hit the streets. Every day I thought *I am not going to hit my children*, and every day I won, until in the end I didn't have to think about it any more. Not hitting was part of me and who I was. Love was what I wanted to give in spades.

I also had the choice to deal with my demons, take medication, go to counselling and seek therapies such as NLP. I made those choices. I come back to my 'every day is a new day' approach from when I was a child. I was damned if I was going to be defined by what had happened to me. I wanted a different future for myself.

Mental health

Suffering mental health issues doesn't always have to signify we are lost forever or weak or fragile. Sure, I do the odd check-in when I ensure I have taken enough rest or question whether I am overdoing it, but it also means not being paranoid about the inevitability of returning to that dark place. Our assumptions can often lead us there, but we can be proved wrong. I went through a time when I'd get a feeling of impending doom as soon as I woke up. The thought of emails – not work ones, but personal ones – coming in made me anxious. I'm not sure what I thought was going to happen, but I was scared of receiving bad news. I then randomly saw Carol Vorderman on TV, who was, bizarrely, explaining exactly the same symptoms I was experiencing, including her sex drive going through the floor. She was saying: "You know, I am too young to feel like this – what is going wrong?" Fast-forward in time and, after a few false starts, I started hormone replacement therapy, and bingo: the symptoms disappeared. Yet I had previously had a conversation with the GP about possibly needing to take antidepressants again. I suspect that might have been the case had I not seen that chance interview.

There can be many reasons for feeling down or depressed that include eating or even not eating certain foods. The trick is to think about the possible reasons and act on them, even experiment with different things and see what happens.

Make the change

I've mentioned forming a new habit. Apparently it takes twenty-one days to do so. I'm not one for gratitude journals, but that isn't to say I don't think they are a good idea. They just aren't my thing. I find it more useful to think about how I can help others rather than feeling grateful for what I have – I am more aware of that. However, in order to make a change, I first have to think about making it, and then action it. Having it in my head is OK but it's no good if I don't actually *do* something. Let's imagine I want to get out of the job I am in and I constantly think about being in a different job. Well, I am not going to get a different job unless I look to see what jobs might be available, update my CV and actually apply. As long as journaling needs to actioning then it definitely gets my vote.

Sometimes when we want a change in behaviour from others, it is necessary to change the way we operate first. I don't mean because they are right, either; I mean it's sometimes the way we act that can generate a change of behaviour in others. It can be in the way you approach something or even think about something. It can be in setting those boundaries and standing up for yourself or physically doing something different. Fear of doing something different is often worse than the outcome of the change we make. It's all in the anticipation. If we could cue dramatic music at the thought of, say, standing up for ourselves, that feeling would result in a physical reaction in our bodies. Sweaty palms, a tight chest, a fluttery stomach. See yourself beyond making the change, really visualise it, notice what you have done and how you have done it. Suddenly the actual event itself will seem less imposing.

Change the story

So often the story we tell ourselves is not the story we want to hear and is most definitely not helpful. We create it from our experiences, culture and learned behaviours. But stories can be recreated and we can be in charge of what that might look like. Like I said, I could have written a story about what had been done 'to me'. Instead, I've focused on my reactions to those things and, where they were negative, I've changed them. So, on the elements of your life that show up as doom and gloom, pick up the pen and a blank sheet of paper and write down what you would like instead. Creating a positive self-fulfilling prophecy rather than a negative one is so much more rewarding.

Do something

Take action. If there are areas of your life you are not happy with, decide what you would like to do, and do something, anything. It doesn't even have to be one of the above; it is your choice. Inaction will result in repeated patterns; ask yourself how well that is working for you right now. Taking action to change the course of your future? Hell, that's powerful and within your gift to control.

Appendix

Some resources I have found helpful on the subjects explored in this book:

Shawn Stevenson podcast – *The Model Health Show*

Dr Rangan Chatterjee podcast – *Feel Better, Live More*

Dr Satchin Panda – his book: *The Circadian Code*

James Clear – his book: *Atomic Habits*

Li-Ju Wang et al. *BMC Genomics* – Fasting and its benefits (available at: ncbi.nlm.nih.gov/pmc/articles/PMC6836141)

Dr Scott Watier and Tommy Welling podcast – *Fasting For Life* (available at: www.thefastingforlife.com)

www.ingramcontent.com/pod-product-compliance
Lightning Source LLC
LaVergne TN
LVHW090115080426
835507LV00040B/900